Green Line 4
Das Trainingsbuch

von
Pauline Ashworth

Klett Lerntraining

Zu diesem Trainingsbuch gehört eine Audio-CD. Mit ihrer Hilfe lernst du, Englisch besser zu verstehen. Die Texte sind im Buch mit dem Symbol gekennzeichnet. Wenn du die Diktate und Lückendiktate schreibst, benutze die Pausentaste, um Zeit zum Schreiben zu haben. Viel Erfolg!

Sprecher: Vanessa Ellmann, Louai Khalil, Isaac McIlvene, Lisa Preuss, Debra Schlipf, Jonathan Tilley, Adrian Turner, Charles Urban, Dominik Vollmer, Amy Walker
Produktion: Ton in Ton Medienhaus, Stuttgart

Bildquellennachweis:
Umschlagfoto U1: Mauritius RF (StockImage), Mittenwald
Umschlagfoto U4: Corbis (Reuters/ Lucy Nicholson), Düsseldorf

Bibliografische Information der Deutschen Nationalbibliothek
Die Deutsche Nationalbibliothek verzeichnet diese Publikation in der Deutschen Nationalbibliografie; detaillierte bibliografische Daten sind im Internet über http://dnb.dnb.de abrufbar.

Auflage 7 | 15

www.klett-lerntraining.de

Redaktion: form & inhalt verlagsservice Martin H. Bredol / Linda Strehl unter Mitarbeit von Louise Carleton-Gertsch
Zeichnungen: Katja Wesner, Fellbach: S. 10, 17, 21, 30, 52, 60, 75, 82, 89, 91, 103, 131; Lars Benecke, Hannover: S. 26, 34, 100; Naomi Fearn, Berlin
Umschlaggestaltung: Koma Amok, Stuttgart
Satz: klartext, Heidelberg
Druck: Grafisches Centrum Cuno GmbH & Co. KG, Calbe (Saale)

Printed in Germany
ISBN 978-3-12-929982-1

9 783129 299821

Inhalt

Zoom-in

The United States 6
Lesen: *Travelling California* 7
Zuhören: *Travelling in the US* 1 9

Unit 1

Pictures 10
New York 10
Abstrakte Substantive 11
Verben 11
Wortfamilien 12
Ort und Zeit 12
Gradadverbien und Adjektive 13
British English und *American English* 14
Wichtige Ausdrücke: Zustimmen oder anderer Meinung sein 14
Das Perfekt und die einfache Form der Vergangenheit (Wiederholung) 15
Die Verlaufsform des Perfekts 16
For und *since* bei der Verlaufsform des Perfekts 17
Das Plusquamperfekt und die einfache Vergangenheit (Wiederholung) 19
Die Verlaufsform des Plusquamperfekts 20
Verben mit Objekt + Adjektiv 22
Adjektive und Adverbien (Wiederholung) 23
Gradadverbien 24
Die Stellung von Adverbien und adverbialen Bestimmungen 25
Present tenses (Wiederholung) 27
Past tenses (Wiederholung) 28
Future tenses (Wiederholung) 29
Lesen: *A famous New York immigrant* 31
Zuhören: *Donald's diner* 2 35
Zuhören: *American pronunciation* 3 35
Hörverstehen: *English in conversations* 36
Conversations 1 4 36
Conversations 2 5 36

Revision A (Unit 1)

Reading: The history of New York City 37
Listening: In a diner 6 40
Writing: A postcard 40
Speaking 41
Mediation 41

Unit 2

People 42
School in the US 42
Politics 43
Verben 43
Wichtige Wendungen 44
British English – American English 45
Adjektive 45
Modale Hilfsverben mit dem Infinitiv Perfekt 46
Der Infinitiv des Passivs ohne *to* 48
Der Infinitiv des Passivs mit *to* 49
Lesen: *Pro and con texts* 51
Lesen und Schreiben: *Pro and con texts* 54
Hörverstehen: *Discussions* 58
Zuhören: *MP3 players in schools 1* 7 58

Zuhören und Sprechen:
MP3 players in schools 2 8 59

Unit 3

Pictures 60
Abstrakte Substantive:
Word formation 60
People and places 61
Verben 62
Adjektive 63
American English vs. British English 63
Wichtige Wendungen:
Small talk/being positive 64
Bedingungssätze (Wiederholung) 65
Das *gerund* als Subjekt und Objekt des Satzes 66
Das *gerund* nach Präpositionen 68
Die Objekt + *-ing*-Form-Konstruktion 70
Das Passiv (Wiederholung) 72
Die Verlaufsformen des Passivs 74
Das Passiv bei Verben mit Präpositionen 76
Grammar skills 77
Lesen: *Love at first sight?* 78
Zuhören und Schreiben:
Small talk 9 82
Zuhören: *American or British?* 10 83

Revision B (Unit 2–3)

Reading: Moving west 84
Listening: Pros and cons of living in the country 11 87
Writing: Sally's e-mail 87
Mediation and speaking:
Small talk 12 88

Unit 4

Bilder 89
Outdoor activities 89
Filme 90
Abstrakte Substantive: Gefühle 90
Adjektive 91
Wichtige Wendungen: Befürchtungen äußern/jemandem helfen 92
Verben 92
Der Infinitiv (Wiederholung) 93
Der Infinitiv mit *to* 94
Gerund oder Infinitiv nach bestimmten Verben 1 96
Gerund oder Infinitiv nach bestimmten Verben 2 97
Zuhören: *In the mountains* 13 98
Indirekte Rede (Wiederholung) 99
Zuhören: *A climbing holiday* 14 100
Lesen: *A movie review* 101
Lesen: *Types of texts* 103
Zuhören: *Expressing fears and being positive* 15 105

Revision C (Unit 4)

Standardprüfung Green Line 3 –
Reading: Tour of the USA 107
Writing and mediation: An e-mail 109
Listening: Telephone messages 16 110
Speaking: Apologising and helping 17 110
Standardprüfung Green Line 4 –
Reading: Skiing in the Rockies 111
Writing: A newspaper report 114
Mediation and speaking: Small talk 115
Listening: Small talk in the mountains 18 115

Unit 5

California 116
Adjektive und Adverbien 117
Verben 118
Phrasal verbs 119
Wichtige Wendungen: *Being polite/ showing feelings* 120

Notwendige Relativsätze (Wiederholung) 121
Nicht-notwendige Relativsätze 122
Komma oder nicht? 19 123
Partizipien als Adjektive 124
Lesen: *The Governor of California* 126
Writing skills: Creative writing 129
Zuhören: *Polite or casual?* 20 131

Lösungen 133

Zoom-in

The United States

1 Trage die Wörter in die richtigen Spalten ein.

capital – cheerleader – flat – house – immigrant – president – scenery – skyscraper – state

buildings	country	people
______	______	______
______	______	______
______	______	______

2 Vervollständige das Kreuzworträtsel.

across:
4. They fly into the air at night and are lots of colours.
7. This is an area of a country, for example.

down:
1. You need this if you want to run a long way, for example.
2. A longer trip.
3. This is a film or a book, for example, which is old but still popular.
4. When you have this, you can do what you want to do and go where you want to.
5. A plant from which flour is made.
6. What you pay somebody when they do something for you.

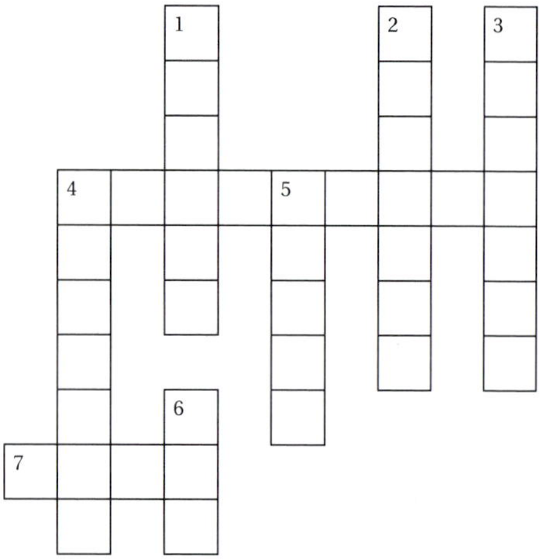

Lesen: *Travelling California*

3 Lies den Text einmal durch, dann beantworte die Fragen dazu: richtig oder falsch?

The US is so large that it is best to concentrate on just one area when you visit, for example, California or Florida. If you want to visit different states then you probably need to fly because of the distances between cities. If you are visiting from Europe, you can buy a special plane ticket which lets you fly as often as you like in one month. There are other ways to travel, though. A lot of people like to do long road journeys and drive from one side of the States to the other. A cheaper way of travelling is to go by bus. Although the buses are often not very comfortable, travelling by bus is a good way to meet other people. There is a railway in America, too, but it is not very good and people do not use it very often.
Here is a short description of one of the main tourist areas. California has something for everybody. It has some interesting cities, for example, San Francisco and Los Angeles, great beaches, and beautiful national parks. The scenery is very varied (*unterschiedlich*): there are high mountains and the hottest, driest valley in the US: Death Valley.
Many people start their journey in San Francisco. Although it is one of the most famous cities in the US, it is only the twelfth biggest. It is most famous for the Golden Gate Bridge and for its cable cars which takes passengers up and down its hills. San Francisco became larger and more important when gold was discovered in California in 1848. It still has many beautiful old buildings that were built around that time. The weather there is often not what many people expect. People usually think that California is hot and sunny, but between November and April it actually often rains in San Francisco. In the summer, it is usually dry, but it is often not hot or sunny, in fact the temperature does not get above 24°C very often and it is sometimes foggy there, too. There are some beaches near San Francisco which are great for surfing but not so good for swimming because the water is cold all through the year.
Los Angeles is the largest city in California. Although many people would say that it is not as beautiful as San Francisco, for anybody interested in film and theatre it is a must-see. You can go to Hollywood and see where famous stars live and if you're lucky, you might even see one or two of them in shops or their favourite cafés.
California is also famous for its national parks, as well as its beautiful countryside and interesting animals and plants. It is home to the tallest trees in the world and and many animals that you can't see in other places. On top of all that there are the beautiful beaches. You can also find some

of the best surfing in the world there. Some of the beaches are empty and others are great for watching all the people there.
All in all California is a place where you can easily spend a month and do lots of different things.

	true	false
1. You can fly as much as you like in a month with a special ticket.	☐	☐
2. Many people use the great railway system in the States.	☐	☐
3. Death Valley is the hottest, driest valley in the US.	☐	☐
4. San Francisco is the twelfth largest city in California.	☐	☐
5. The weather is always sunny and hot in San Francisco.	☐	☐
6. People who love films should visit Los Angeles.	☐	☐
7. All Californian beaches are empty.	☐	☐

4 Lies den Text ein zweites Mal und beantworte dann die folgenden Fragen.

1. How many different names can you find for America in the text? ________
2. What are the names? ________
3. What is a cheaper way to travel than by car in the US? ________
4. What is San Francisco famous for? ________
5. When was gold discovered in California? ________
6. When does it rain a lot in San Francisco? ________

Zuhören: *Travelling in the US* 1

5 Höre dir zunächst auf der CD an, was Mary, Jill und Cathie über ihre Ferien in den USA erzählen. Dann lies dir die folgenden Notizen durch. Wer hat wo seine Ferien verbracht?

1.	2.	3.
Flew to California.	Did road journey from New York to San Francisco.	Flew to New York.
Drove around the state.	Visited Chicago and Great Lakes.	Spent a week in New York.
Visited San Francisco.	Drove through Rocky Mountains.	Visited Washington and New England.
Visited Yosemite National Park.	Visited Yellowstone National Park.	Flew to Arizona and visited Grand Canyon.
Drove through Death Valley.	Finished in San Francisco.	Flew to San Francisco.
Drove to coast.	Went surfing.	Spent a week on the beach.
Went swimming in sea.		Flew home again.
Finished in Los Angeles.		
→ ____________	→ ____________	→ ____________

6 Unterstreiche die richtigen Wörter. Dann höre dir CD-Track 1 noch einmal an und überprüfe, ob du richtig liegst.

1. Mary flew around the States on her week's/month's plane ticket which she bought on the Internet/in a shop. She walked/flew in a helicopter through the Grand Canyon. At the end she flew back to London/New York.
2. Jill wanted to do a road trip but didn't because she didn't have enough time/money. She liked Yosemite but thought Death Valley/Yellowstone was better.
3. Cathie went on her first/third road trip across the States. She loved Yellowstone/Nevada and they sold the car in San Francisco. She sometimes/often/never felt that she never wanted to get in a car again.

Unit 1

Pictures

1 Schau dir die Bilder an und beschrifte sie korrekt.

1. ______________ 2. ______________ 3. ______________ 4. ______________

New York

2 Lies den Lückentext über New York und ergänze die passenden Wörter.

drugs – gate – grandparents – immigrants – neighbours – weeds – yard

Sandro lives in New York. His parents were ______________ from Italy but he was born in America. His ______________ still live in Italy and he often goes there. Sandro lives in Little Italy, the Italian part of town, and his ______________ speak Italian, too, although the younger people speak English to each other. Last year they moved into a small house with a ______________ behind. It was full of ______________ and had a small ______________ which didn't lock. Why hadn't the last people looked after it, he wondered. Sandro was trying to get rid of the weeds when a policeman came past and asked, "Did you plant those?" – "What? These weeds?" asked Sandro surprised. The policeman laughed. "They aren't weeds. They're ______________," he said.

Abstrakte Substantive

3 Löse die Buchstabenrätsel auf und ordne sie der richtigen Übersetzung zu.

icecho **pineshaps** **pressimion** **eacep** **surepres** **pathsymy**

Glück	______________	Wahl	______________
Druck	______________	Mitleid	______________
Eindruck	______________	Frieden	______________

Verben

4 Umzug nach New York. Setze die angegebenen Verben im *simple past* ein.

drop out – happen to – do well – look around – notice – push – recognize – say goodbye – serve

Jane ______________ at school but she ______________ of college because she found it boring. She ______________ to her friends at home and moved to New York. She ______________ for a job but couldn't find one at first. But then, while she was walking through Manhattan, she ______________ see an ad in the window of a diner. She went in to ask for the job but the diner was full. After some time she ______________ that only one person was working there and he was tired out. She watched for some time and saw how things were done. Then she ______________ her way through the crowd, went behind the counter and ______________ for the rest of the day. She was serving one customer when she suddenly ______________ him. It was a famous actor. But it couldn't be him, could it? Yes, this was New York and anything was possible.

Wortfamilien

5 Leite von dem jeweils angegebenen Wort die passenden, zur selben Wortfamilie gehörigen Wörter ab oder verwende das bereits angegebene Wort.

1. **lucky:** You need a lot of ______________ to win 1000 dollars. I won it but I was ______________ because I lost it before I spent it.
2. **hope:** I love skateboarding but I'm ______________ at it. ______________ I'll learn something at the skateboard park this afternoon.
3. **immigrant:** There are still many ______________ in New York but there is not as much ______________ now.
4. **happy:** She has been very ______________ since she met him and you can see her ______________ in her smile.

Ort und Zeit

6 Gäste in einem Schnellrestaurant. Ergänze die passenden Wendungen.

at any time – ages ago – at the back of – for – since – over here

1. "I came in here ______________ and I still haven't been served."
2. "I'm too small. Nobody can see me ______________ the queue."
3. "This place is always full. There's a queue ______________ of day."
4. "I've been waiting ______________ ages."
5. "Two bagels and a coffee to go?" – "______________, please."
6. "I love this place. I've been coming here ______________ I was six."

Gradadverbien und Adjektive

7 Bei einem Fest in New York. Unterstreiche die Gradadverbien, die passen.
Tipp: Es können mehrere richtig sein!

1. I enjoyed the party very much/really/pretty.

2. I really/too/extremely loved the music.

3. The food was extremely/very much/really delicious.

4. I met a girl there who was pretty/very/very much exciting.

5. But she was completely/very much/too much hopeless at dancing.

6. But I very good/quite/extremely enjoyed meeting her.

7. Unfortunately I completely/very/too forgot that my girlfriend was there, too.

8 Suche aus der Wortschlange die Adjektive heraus und ergänze sie in den richtigen Lücken.

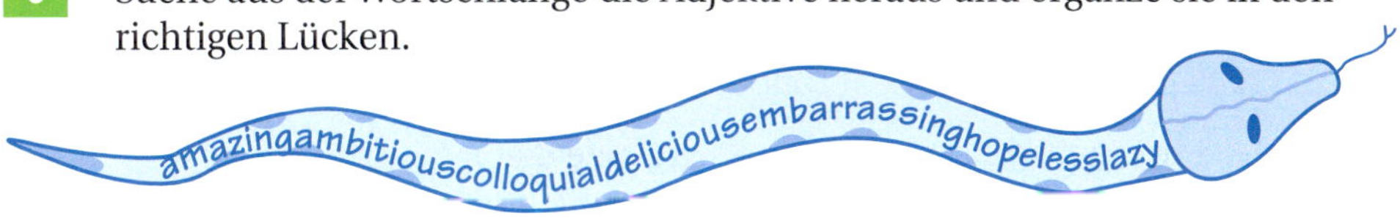

That food tastes very, very good. It's ________________.

He really wants to be best at everything. He's very ________________.

I love painting pictures, but I'm really bad at it. I'm ________________.

She never works at anything. She's very ________________.

The garden was all weeds last year but it's beautiful now. That's

________________.

That book is difficult to read because the language is so ________________.

I fell off my chair. It was very ________________.

British English und *American English*

9 Wie lauten die britischen Begriffe jeweils im *American English?* Ändere Wort oder Schreibweise.

1. underground ____________
2. taxi ____________
3. holiday ____________
4. city centre ____________
5. flat ____________
6. sweets ____________
7. storey ____________
8. programme ____________
9. neighbourhood ____________
10. theatre ____________
11. bill ____________
12. rubbish ____________
13. toilet ____________
14. trousers ____________

Wichtige Wendungen: Zustimmen oder anderer Meinung sein

10 Was könnte man in diesen Situationen sagen? Vervollständige.

1. I've got so much work at school but I really need to help the guys with the mural. – I w________ I c________ h________ but I'm terrible at painting.
2. My cousins are coming again this summer from England. – Oh, great. I_____ r__________ l__________ f__________ to meeting them.
3. My dad had a car crash and he's in hospital now. I'm very worried about him. – H_______ t____________!
4. Guess what! I've won the mural competition. I'm going to meet some top mural artists next week. – T________ a__________ng! – Yes, it's t_______ br__________ f_______ w_________ds.

Das Perfekt und die einfache Form der Vergangenheit (Wiederholung)

Du verwendest das ***present perfect,*** wenn eine Handlung etwas mit dem *present* (Gegenwart) zu tun hat, wenn also die Auswirkung noch spürbar ist:

She**'s met** her favourite actor. She's still on top of the world.

They**'ve worked** all night and they're tired.

Du verwendest das ***present perfect*** auch, wenn du sagen willst, dass etwas passiert ist, was noch von Bedeutung ist, aber ohne Zeitpunkt genannt wird:

He**'s been** to New York a few times. (Es ist wichtig, *dass* er New York besucht hat, aber nicht, *wann*.)

Du verwendest das ***simple past,*** wenn du sagen möchtest, wann etwas passiert ist:

He **visited** New York last year.

Wenn du über etwas Bestimmtes redest, das in der Vergangenheit passiert ist, verwendest du ebenfalls das ***simple past,*** auch wenn du nicht ausdrücklich angibst, wann es passiert ist:

She has finished the mural. She **worked** really hard at it.

Signalwörter für das *present perfect:* never, ever, so far, already, yet, just; für das *simple past:* yesterday, in 2009, … ago, when

11 Johns Erlebnisse in New York. Ergänze die richtigen Zeitformen.

John ______________ (arrive) in New York yesterday. He ______________ (never/be) to America before, so he's very excited. He's staying with his girlfriend, Janet. She ______________ (live) in New York for six months and ______________ (not/see) everything yet. They ______________ (just/take) an elevator to the top of the Empire State Building. Jane ______________ (be) up before but the weather ______________ (not/be) very good then so she couldn't see much. Today the view is excellent and they can see the whole of New York, but, oh no, John ______________ (forget) his camera.

Die Verlaufsform des Perfekts

Mit dem ***present perfect progressive*** beschreibst du eine Handlung, die in der Vergangenheit angefangen und noch nicht aufgehört hat:

I'**ve been waiting** for the bus for twenty minutes. (I arrived at the bus stop twenty minutes ago and I'm still waiting now.)

Louise **has been living** in New York for three years. (She moved to New York three years ago and still lives here now.)

What **have** you **been doing?** You look tired.

– Das *present perfect progressive* wird mit ***have been/has been*** und dem ***present participle*** gebildet.

– Es wird oft mit dem Präsens und „schon" übersetzt, z. B.: Louise wohnt schon seit drei Jahren in New York.

– Das *present perfect progressive* betont die Dauer einer Handlung, die in der Vergangenheit angefangen hat und noch nicht zu Ende ist. Man kann es oft wie das *present perfect* verwenden:

He'**s worked** in this diner for two months ≈ He'**s been working** in this diner for two months.

12 In einem *diner*. Gib die Sätze mit dem *present perfect progressive* wieder.

1. John started work at 8 am. He's still working now.

   → John ________________________________ since 8 am.

2. Ella started to eat her lunch an hour ago and she's still eating now.

   → Ella ________________________________ her lunch for an hour.

3. I ordered my lunch twenty minutes ago. I'm still waiting for it now.

   → I ________________________________ for lunch for twenty minutes.

4. Dave and Alice came in at 11:00. They were having an argument. They are still having an argument.

   → Dave and Alice ________________________________ an argument since 11:00.

For und *since* bei der Verlaufsform des Perfekts

Wenn du sagen willst, wie lange eine Handlung schon andauert, verwendest du ***for*** oder ***since.***

For verwendest du mit einem Zeitraum (z. B. *three months, two minutes, ages, a long time*):

I've been waiting here **for** half an hour.

Since verwendest du mit einem Zeitpunkt (z. B. *8 o'clock, 1997, my birthday, I moved to New York*):

I've been playing the piano **since** 1997.

I've been working in this diner **since** I moved to New York.

Wenn man *since* mit einem Nebensatz verwendet, z.B. *I moved to New York*, verwendet man das *simple past*.

13 Wie lange dauern die Handlungen auf den Bildern jeweils schon an?

1. Alice ____

____.

8 o'clock

to play the guitar

John arrived

to draw

2. John ____

____.

14 Drei Uhr in New York. Was passiert seit wann? Verwende die angegebenen Wörter, um vollständige Sätze im *present perfect progressive* zu bilden.

1. What – they – do – ?

____

2. Miguel – work – seven hours

____

3. Tina and her friends – dance – half past ten

____

15 Trage die Verben in der richtigen Form (*present perfect simple* oder *progressive, simple past*) sowie *for* oder *since* ein.

I _______________ (work) in this diner _______ I _______________ (come) to New York two years ago. I _______________ (serve) thousands of customers and I know some of them quite well. Some _______________ (come) in here _______ I _______________ (start) to work here. There's old Antonia. She _______________ (live) in New York _______ sixty-five years and she still speaks Italian better than English. Then there's Chan. He _______________ (try) every single sandwich and bagel we have in here and often gives us new ideas. And then there's William. He _______________ (come) here _______ my boss _______________ (open) the café and he _______________ (never/pay) for a bagel once. But then as my boss _______________ (often/say) dogs don't need to pay.

Das Plusquamperfekt und die einfache Vergangenheit (Wiederholung)

Das ***past perfect simple*** verwendest du, wenn du sagen oder betonen willst, dass etwas vor etwas anderem in der Vergangenheit passiert ist:

When I arrived at the party, it **had** already **finished.** (The party finished first and then I arrived there.)

The garden looked great because they **had worked** hard. (They worked hard and then the garden looked great.)

Man bildet das *past perfect simple* mit ***had*** und dem ***past participle.*** Es wird meist zusammen mit dem *simple past* verwendet:

I got up and went downstairs. I felt tired because I **hadn't slept** well.

16 *The garden party.* Lies den Text und vervollständige die Lücken mit der richtigen Verbform in *simple past* oder *past perfect.*

The garden looked wonderful. It ____________ (be) hard work but it was worth it. It ____________ (take) over a year to finish, but the garden ____________ (be) now a nice place to relax in. First they ____________ (take) out the weeds and then they ____________ (plant) some trees. It ____________ (be) fun and now it was finished so they ____________ (want) to have a big party to show everybody what they ____________ (do). The party was on Saturday and they were all very excited when they ____________ (arrive). But when they ____________ (go) in, they got a shock. Somebody ____________ (pull) lots of flowers out of the ground. They were angry. Who ____________ (do) it? Then they found out. Two foxes ____________ (move) into the garden over night. "Well, we wanted to share our garden," laughed Marie.

Die Verlaufsform des Plusquamperfekts

Du verwendest das *past perfect progressive*, wenn du ausdrücken willst, wie lange etwas bis zu einem bestimmten Punkt in der Vergangenheit passiert ist:

Paul **had been waiting** for 20 minutes when his friend arrived. – Paul hatte (schon) 20 Minuten gewartet, als (endlich) sein Freund kam.

We **had been living** in San Francisco for three years before we moved to New York. – Wir wohnten drei Jahre lang in San Francisco, bevor wir nach New York zogen.

I **had been working** hard all day so I didn't want to go out later. – Ich hatte den ganzen Tag hart gearbeitet, deshalb wollte ich später nicht ausgehen.

She **had been learning** English since she was six and so she could speak it quite well. – Sie lernte Englisch, seit sie sechs war, daher konnte sie es ziemlich gut.

17 *A special day in the diner.* Lies den Text und trage die Verben in der richtigen Zeitform ein: *past perfect progressive* oder *simple past?*

Alice ______________________ (clean) the diner for an hour when some friends arrived. They ______________________ (shop) since the shops ______________________ (open). When everything was ready, Alice and her friends ______________________ (prepare) food for an hour. When Diego ______________________ (arrive) at his diner, everybody ______________________ (hide) under the tables for a few minutes. When everybody ______________________ (shout), "Happy Birthday Diego", he ______________________ (wonder) where everybody was.

18 *Yesterday at 8 am in a skyscraper.* Schau dir die Bilder an und formuliere Sätze im *past perfect progressive,* die sie beschreiben.

all night

1. Mac and his brother ___ films ___.

7 o'clock

2. A man ___.

19 *Yesterday in Central Park.* Übersetze die Sätze ins Englische.

1. Ich joggte schon eine halbe Stunde, als ich einen berühmten Schauspieler sah.

___

2. Jenny suchte den Zoo ewig, bevor sie ihn fand.

___

3. Du hattest ein Buch gelesen, als es zu regnen anfing.

___

Verben mit Objekt + Adjektiv

Es gibt bestimmte Verben, auf die ein direktes Objekt und ein Adjektiv folgen kann:

I **find New York exciting.** – Ich finde, dass New York spannend ist.

Diego always tries to **make his food delicious.** – Diego versucht immer, sein Essen lecker zu machen.

20 Ein Besuch in New York. Bilde ganze Sätze in der richtigen Reihenfolge.

almost – happy – I – everybody – see – love – to

find – the – friendly – people – I

nervous – me – the – subway – makes

people – streets – we – like – full – the – of

21 *In a restaurant.* Übersetze die folgende Sätze.

1. Der Duft des Essens macht mich immer hungrig.

2. Sie kochen ihre Speisen immer frisch.

3. Der Chef hat es gern, wenn er die Gäste immer glücklich machen kann. (Tipp: *like* + *keep* + *guests* + Adjektiv)

Adjektive und Adverbien (Wiederholung)

Du verwendest **Adverbien,** um auszudrücken, wie etwas getan wird. Mit **Adjektiven** beschreibst du, wie etwas *ist:* He **cooks well.** He's a **good cook.**

Man verwendet Adjektive nach Verben, die einen Zustand angeben: The food **tastes good.** It **smells delicious.**

Adverbien stehen meist nach dem Objekt oder Verb: He eats **curry quickly.**

Du bildest die meisten Adverbien, indem du an das Adjektiv ***-ly*** hängst. Achte auf folgende Schreibregeln:

Adjektiv	Adverb	
hopeless	**hopelessly**	*+ -ly*
awful	**awfully**	*-ful* → *-fully*
lazy	**lazily**	*-y* nach Konsonant → *-ily*
horrible	**horribly**	*-le* → *-ly*

Es gibt auch ein paar Ausnahmen: good – **well;** fast – **fast;** hard – **hard;** friendly – **in a friendly way**

22 New York. Ergänze die angegebenen Wörter in der richtigen Form: Brauchst du das Adjektiv oder das Adverb?

New York is an ______ (exciting) place and some people call it ______ (beautiful). A lot of people live and work in a very ______ (small) area so the streets and shops are often ______ (full). But you can do anything in New York: skate ______ (fast) in Central Park or sail ______ (slow) in the harbour. You can eat ______ (good) in one of the thousands of restaurants or eat ______ (cheap) in a diner. But there's maybe one thing you can't do in New York: get ______ (bored)!

Gradadverbien

Wenn man ein Adjektiv, ein Adverb oder Verb verstärken oder abschwächen möchte, verwendet man **Gradadverbien.** Sie stehen normalerweise **vor** dem Wort, das sie ändern sollen:

I'm **really** hungry.

The tea is **too** cold.

I've **almost** finished my homework.

He runs **quite** fast.

Manche verstärkende Adverbien können auch **am Satzende** stehen, wenn man sie betonen möchte:

Great! He's finished **completely.**

Manche müssen am Satzende stehen:

He hurt me **very much.**

Andere Gradadverbien sind ***quite, pretty, very, extremely.***

23 Formuliere die Sätze neu, indem du sie wie gefordert veränderst.

1. It's nice.

(abgeschwächt) ______

(verstärkt) ______

(weiter verstärkt) ______

2. I like it.

(abgeschwächt) ______

(verstärkt) ______

3. She sings well.

(abgeschwächt) ______

(verstärkt) ______

(weiter verstärkt) ______

4. I've finished.

(abgeschwächt) ______

(verstärkt) ______

Die Stellung von Adverbien und adverbialen Bestimmungen

Es gibt Adverbien der Häufigkeit und der Art und Weise sowie adverbiale Bestimmungen des Ortes und der Richtung. Abhängend von der Art der Adverbien können sie in *front position* (vor dem Subjekt), *midposition* (vor dem Vollverb) oder *end position* (hinter dem Verb und Objekt) stehen.

– ***Adverbs of frequency*** (z. B. *often, never*) stehen meistens in *mid position:*

I **often** eat bagels. (zwischen Subjekt und Verb)

I have **never** eaten bagels. (zwischen Hilfsverb und Verb)

Sometimes kann auch in *front position* stehen:

Sometimes I go to town on Fridays.

– ***Adverbs of manner*** (z. B. *carefully, well*) stehen meist in *end position,* können auch aber in *mid position* stehen:

He walks **slowly.**

He **slowly** walked across the room.

– ***Adverbials of time and place*** (z. B. *on Fridays, in town*) stehen meist in *end position,* können aber auch, vor allem zur Betonung, in *front position* stehen:

I work **in town.**

On Fridays I eat fish.

Wenn mehrere *adverbials of time and place* am Ende eines Satzes stehen, kommt das *adverbial of place* zuerst:

I often go **to town on Friday.** (Ort vor Zeit!)

Wenn mehrere *adverbials of time* am Ende eines Satzes stehen, kommt das spezifischere zuerst:

I always go to bed **at 9 at the weekend.**

24 In New York. Unterstreiche die *adverbs* und *adverbials* und gib die Art an.

1. Many people eat in diners.

2. You can easily find your way around New York.

3. We've always lived in Little Italy.

4. Times Square is busy at night.

25 Bilde aus den angegebenen Wörtern vollständige Sätze in der richtigen Wortstellung.

1. in Germany – in 1991 – was born – Mustafa

____

2. been – had – always – interested – he – in the States

____

3. he – in – to – the US – 2009 – moved

____

4. speak – didn't – at – first – very – well – English – he

____

5. happily – has – lived – in – Mustafa – July – year – New York – since – last

____

26 Formuliere den Satz neu, indem du ihn jeweils mit den angegebenen Wörtern erweiterst, bis zuletzt alle Adverbien im Satz vorkommen.

(+ in a diner) ____________________

(+ on Saturdays) ________________________

(+ happily) ____________________________

(+ at lunchtime) __________________________________

(+ in New York) ______________________________________

(+ often) ____

Present tenses (Wiederholung)

Sprichst du über etwas, das
– immer wahr ist, regelmäßig passiert oder in einer Geschichte nacheinander passiert, verwendest du das ***simple present:***
I often **eat** in a diner.
– vorübergehend ist, verwendest du das ***present progressive:***
I**'m eating** dinner now.

27 In Little Italy. Ergänze die richtige Form der Gegenwart.

I ____ (live) in Little Italy and I work in an Italian restaurant. My parents are Italian and I ____ (look) Italian but I ____ (not/speak) Italian. This is a problem because guests often ____ (come) in and speak to me in Italian and I ____ (not/understand) a word. My boss is American, but he ____ (speak) Italian. He ____ (feel) Italian he says. "What ____ (it/feel) like?" I ask but he ____ (not/reply). I've decided to learn Italian and so now I ____ (stay) at my grandparents' house near Rome. I ____ (try) to cross a road now. Everybody ____ (drive) past me and I can't cross. These Italians are crazy. Teenagers ____ (drive) their mopeds in and out of the traffic. Why ____ (they/not/crash)? A woman ____ (come) and crosses the road before me. She just ____ (walk) into the road and the cars drive around her. These Italians are crazy and I love them.

Past tenses (Wiederholung)

Simple past: Etwas passiert zu einem bestimmten Zeitpunkt in der Vergangenheit:

Yesterday I **went** to Central Park.

Present perfect: Etwas mit einer Verbindung zur Gegenwart passiert in der Vergangenheit:

I**'ve been** to New York twice.

Past perfect: Etwas passiert vor einem bestimmten Zeitpunkt in der Vergangenheit:

The party **had** already **started** when I arrived.

Past progressive: Etwas dauert zu einem bestimmten Zeitpunkt in der Vergangenheit an:

He **was eating** in a diner at 6 pm.

Present perfect progressive: Etwas dauert bis jetzt an:

I**'ve been eating** lunch for the last hour.

Past perfect progressive: Etwas dauert bis zu einem Zeitpunkt in der Vergangenheit an:

I**'d been eating** lunch for an hour when he phoned.

28 New York ist ein Dorf. Unterstreiche die richtige Zeitform.

New York is very big and yesterday I was glad because I wanted/had wanted some time alone to think about the future. But then I walked/was walking through Central Park when I met a friend, Zak. He just met/had just met another friend of ours, Pamela. Pamela has been skating/had been skating all morning around the park but I hadn't seen her. Zak and I were talking when we saw/had seen Gina, too. Gina looked/was looking for Pamela but couldn't find her. I was living/'ve been living in New York for two years and I've never met anybody I know by chance. So why was everybody/had everybody been in Central Park that day? Then I found out. There was a free concert with lots of stars that afternoon.

Future tenses (Wiederholung)

Will future: Etwas wird in der Zukunft passieren, aber man kann es nicht planen; man glaubt, dass es passieren wird; spontane Entscheidungen:

I'**ll be** 15 tomorrow.

I hope **I'll get** lots of presents.

The phone's ringing. I'**ll answer** it.

Going to future: Jemand hat etwas geplant oder sieht Anzeichen für etwas, das passieren wird:

John **is going to move** to New York next year.

Watch out. You'**re going to fall.**

Present progressive: Es handelt sich um Vereinbarungen in der näheren Zukunft; etwas ist mit jemandem abgesprochen:

I'**m meeting** Sue later.

Simple present: Es handelt sich um einen festen Termin in der Zukunft, z. B. einen *timetable:*

His flight **arrives** at six.

Future perfect: Etwas passiert vor einem bestimmten Zeitpunkt in der Zukunft:

He **will have landed** by this time tomorrow.

29 Vorbereitungen zu einer Party. Lies die Sätze und vervollständige die Dialoge.

1. What food should we buy? – Well, we ______ (make) a big pizza. – OK. I ______ (get) some cheese and tomatoes.
2. Do you think we should eat outside? – No, I think it ______ (be) too cold.
3. Where's Henry? Isn't he coming? – Yes, but his train ______ (not/arrive) until half past six. – Oh, he ______ (arrive) then by now. It's already six forty.

30 Im Central Park. Schau dir die Bilder und Sätze an. Es ist jetzt ein Uhr. Welche Sätze passen zu den Bildern? Nenne die Buchstaben.

Correct sentences: ___

12:00

13:00

a) A man has fallen off his bike.
b) A man fell off his bike at midday.
c) A family is tidying up.
d) A family tidies up.
e) A family has had a picnic.
f) A family had had a picnic.
g) A boy waited for somebody.
h) A boy has been waiting for somebody for an hour.
i) A boy is waiting for somebody.
j) A girl bought an ice cream at 12.
k) A girl has bought an ice cream.
l) A girl is going to play tennis.
m) A girl is playing tennis.

31 Besuch in New York. Trage die angegebenen Verben in der richtigen Zeitform ein.

This time tomorrow I ___ (leave) New York. I will be on a plane back to England. I ___ (have) a great time here and it's funny to think I ___ (not/want) to come here at all. I only ___ (come) because my best friend had immigrated to New York the summer before. She ___ (love) it here and I think she ___ never/leave). And me? I ___ (live) here one day, too.

Lesen: *A famous New York immigrant*

32 Lies den Text einmal zügig durch. Welche Überschriften passen zu welchen Abschnitten? Ergänze die Ziffern.

a) Life is hard in Ireland **b) Frank goes home** **c) Making money**

d) Frank's parents go home **e) Keeping warm**

a) ________; b) ________; c) ________; d) ________; e) ________

Tipp Wenn du einen unbekannten Text vor dir hast, ist es sinnvoll, ihn einmal zügig durchzulesen, um eine Vorstellung davon zu bekommen, wovon er handelt. Du brauchst nicht sofort jedes einzelne Wort zu verstehen.

1. Frank's parents were Irish immigrants who lived in New York. They had left Ireland because life was so hard there, but life was hard in New York, too. It was difficult to find work and Frank's father spent their money on drink. Frank was born in 1930 and his parents had three more sons in the next two years. A girl was born in 1935, but she died only a few weeks later. Times were bad in the States, so the whole family went back to Ireland where they hoped life would be easier. It wasn't!

2. When they arrived back in Ireland, they had to live in a house with an outside toilet that half the people in the street shared. It was not clean and they often got ill. Frank's younger twin brothers died in their first year back. His dad mostly didn't work and when he did find work, he usually spent any money he was paid on drink. Frank's mother, Angela, was not able to buy the family many clothes or much food. She was given money by the church, but they never had enough food and so they were never healthy. Frank got ill and had to go to hospital. He was lucky because he recovered. Angela had two more sons before their father left to work in England in the 1940s. He only sent money back once and Angela was worse off than before.

3. Frank and his brothers sometimes had to steal coal (*Kohle*) to burn on the fire and food to eat, so they tried to find work as soon as they could. One winter Frank cut down some of the wood in the house to burn on the fire because it was so cold. But the wood had held the roof up and the roof fell down, so they could not live there anymore. They moved into another house with a relative, but life was not better there.

4. Frank went to school until he was 13 and learnt to read and write well. When he left school, he got a job with the post office and he also worked for a money lender who lived near them. She lent money to people which they had to pay back again later plus some extra. If they didn't have any money, the woman wrote letters to them to make them pay it back. She wasn't very good at it, so Frank wrote the letters for her. He made the poor people scared and that way he earned some more money for himself. Now he was able to save a little. Frank wanted to save money because he had a dream: to go back to New York. Although life had been difficult there, Frank had always thought it was an exciting place. When he was 19 he had saved enough money to buy a one-way ticket to New York.

5. There were lots of immigrants in New York at this time and life was not easy. Frank had no friends there and no idea how to find a job. He was lucky at one point and got a job in a hotel. Later he joined the US army and was sent back to Europe – to Germany. He earned lots of money there and later went back to New York. Things were getting easier for him now and after a few years he became a student at New York University. That was possible because he had been in the army. He then became a teacher and taught English at school, college and at university. After he had worked for a few years, he paid for his mother and brothers to join him in New York. For many years he had wanted to write a book about his life, but he waited until his mother died. When he was 69, Frank McCourt finished his first book and soon after became very famous. People loved his book and after a few years it was made into a film, "Angela's Ashes".

33 Informationen finden: Lies den Text noch einmal und beantworte die folgenden Fragen dazu.

1. Where was Frank born? ______
2. When was he born? ______
3. Where did Frank's dad find work? ______
4. Why did they have to move out of their house? ______
5. How long did Frank go to school? ______
6. What was Frank's dream? ______
7. How old was Frank when he went back to New York? ______
8. What did Frank McCourt teach? ______

34 Lies den Text nochmals genau durch, dann sieh dir die folgenden Sätze an: Sind sie *true, false* oder *not in the text?* Korrigiere dann die Sätze, die falsch sind.

	true	false	not in the text
1. Frank's parents were born in Ireland.	☐	☐	☐
2. Frank's twin brothers died at the same time.	☐	☐	☐
3. Frank's dad sent money back from England.	☐	☐	☐
4. Angela gave money to the church.	☐	☐	☐
5. The roof fell down because Frank cut down some wood.	☐	☐	☐
6. The money lender paid Frank to write horrible letters.	☐	☐	☐
7. When Frank sailed back to New York, he had five brothers.	☐	☐	☐
8. Frank never wanted to move to Europe.	☐	☐	☐

Korrektur: ______________________________

____

35 Vervollständige die folgenden Sätze mit Informationen aus dem Text.

1. Frank wanted to burn some wood to ______________________.
2. Frank wrote some letters to try and make ______________________.
3. Frank found New York ______________________.
4. He ______________________ for a few years when he paid for his family to join him in New York.

36 Frank stiehlt und schreibt Drohbriefe. Lies die folgenden Meinungen dazu und schreibe die Wendungen heraus, die die Schreiber verwendet haben, um ihre Meinung auszudrücken.

1. "I don't believe it's OK to steal usually, but I don't see what else you can do if you are very hungry. If you didn't steal then, you would just die. But I really don't think it's OK to write letters to poor people to make them scared. They were poor people, just like Frank. If you ask me, he should have helped them and not the rich money lender who wanted their money."

I don't believe …

2. "Personally, I find it terrible that he stole and that he made people scared. If things are difficult for you, that's no reason to make things difficult for other people."

3. "In my opinion he didn't do anything wrong. He didn't really hurt anybody and he paid for his family to come to America. I believe anybody would do the same."

37 Schau dir Alisons Gedanken an und formuliere, was sie denkt. Verwende dazu die Wendungen, die du in Übung 36 herausgeschrieben hast.

I believe that everybody would steal if

Zuhören: *Donald's diner* 2

38 Donalds *diner* ist sehr voll. Wie versuchen die Gäste, auf sich aufmerksam zu machen? Höre dir die Dialoge an und notiere jeweils den Satz.

1. ____________________
2. ____________________
3. ____________________
4. ____________________
5. ____________________

Zuhören: *American pronunciation* 3

39 Höre dir die Sätze an. Welche sind in britischem *(BE)*, welche in amerikanischem Englisch *(AE)* gesprochen?

1. ______ 3. ______ 5. ______ 7. ______ 9. ______

2. ______ 4. ______ 6. ______ 8. ______ 10. ______

40 Höre dir CD-Track 3 nochmals an und schreibe die amerikanischen Sätze aus.

1. ____________________
2. ____________________
3. ____________________
4. ____________________
5. ____________________

Hörverstehen: *English in conversations*

Das Wichtigste heraushören: Schlüsselwörter
Auch Muttersprachler verstehen manchmal nicht jedes Wort, das gesprochen wird. Hörverstehen ist Übungssache: Wenn du oft genug englische Texte hörst, lernst du, das Wichtigste herauszuhören.

Unterbrechen
Wenn es trotzdem passiert, dass du das Wesentliche verpasst, fragst du einfach nach: I'm sorry. Could you repeat that, please?

Unterschiedliche Aussprache
Es hilft, wenn du weißt, welche sprachlichen Unterschiede es gibt. Im amerikanischen Englisch wird [ɑ:] oft als [æ] (z. B. in *half*) und [t] oft als [d] (z. B. in *little*) ausgesprochen.

Conversations 1 4

41 Höre dir den Anfang der Dialoge an. Welcher der hier angegebenen Sätze wird in welchem Dialog vermutlich als nächster gesprochen?

a) Sorry! What is that?
b) I'm sorry. What is a pastrami, please?
c) I'm afraid I didn't understand anything.
d) I'm sorry. I didn't hear you. Could you repeat that, please?
e) Do you think you could speak more slowly, please?
f) Do you think you could speak more clearly, please?

1. ________
2. ________
3. ________

Conversations 2 5

42 Höre dir nun die vollständigen Dialoge an und überprüfe deine Antworten zu Übung 41. Dann beantworte die folgenden Fragen.

1. What does the woman suggest? ______________________________

2. In which street is the Hollywood Diner? ______________________________

3. The boy should walk down Christopher Street until he reaches which street? ______________________________

4. What does the boy order? ______________________________

Revision A (Unit 1)

Reading: The history of New York City

1 Lies zunächst den Text durch. Dann ordne den Absatzüberschriften am Ende jeweils einen Buchstaben zu.

A. The Dutch first built a village where New York is in 1624, but before that Native Americans had been living there for centuries. The Dutch actually bought Manhattan Island from the Native Americans and they called their village New Amsterdam. After the English had fought the Dutch in 1664 and had taken New Amsterdam, they called it New York.

B. Not long after the United States of America had become independent from England in 1783, New York became its capital. When New York became America's largest city in 1790, George Washington was already the President.

C. In the 19th century many people started to move to New York from different European countries. They often left their own countries because they did not have enough to eat. This is the reason why many Irish people came to America in 1845. Other people left their countries because they were treated badly because of their religious beliefs. At first people landed in Manhattan when they arrived, but in 1892 the immigration station there was closed and a new one was opened on Ellis Island. The first immigrant there was a young Irish girl.

D. By the time the immigration station on Ellis Island closed in 1954, millions of people had landed there. They had all had terrible journeys on ships and many people had died on the way. Starting in 1921 only a certain number of people were allowed in from some countries each day. This meant that, for example, when the maximum number of Polish people had already been allowed in that day, the next Polish person was sent home. One time a Polish woman had a baby on the ship on her way to America. She was the last Polish person to be allowed in to New York that day so her baby was not allowed in. Luckily a man had an idea and decided that her baby was not Polish but was American. There is now a museum at Ellis Island where you can find out about immigration to America.

E. Starting in 1886 all the immigrants who landed in New York sailed past the Statue of Liberty. The statue was a present from France to celebrate the fact that America had been independent for 100 years. It is a symbol of freedom and many immigrants must have felt that America was their only chance of freedom at that time. The statue is on Liberty Island and you can go inside the statue's head and crown and get a great view of New York's waterfront.

F. Modern New York City was created out of Manhattan Island, Brooklyn, Queens, parts of the Bronx and some of Richmond, now Staten Island, in 1898. The New York City subway opened in 1904 and helped the city to grow together. When New York City was created, over three million people lived there. The number of people had been growing since 1700 when the population there was first counted. Now over eight million people live in the city and over thirty-six per cent of them were born in foreign countries.

___ New York gets a present	___ New York becomes a city
___ New York becomes English	___ Immigration stations
___ A difficult time for immigrants	___ The first American President

2 Stelle die Ereignisse aus dem Text in die chronologisch richtige Reihenfolge, indem du sie nummerierst.

___ The US became independent from England.

___ The New York Subway was opened. F

___ The immigration station moved to Ellis Island.

5 George Washington became President of the United States.

___ New York was given the Statue of Liberty by France. E

___ Modern New York City was created with its five boroughs. F

___ New York first became American's largest city. A

___ The immigration station at Ellis Island was closed.

1 The Dutch bought Manhattan Island from the Native Americans.

___ New York became the capital of America.

___ The British took the island from the Dutch.

3 Sind die folgenden Aussagen *true, false* oder *not in the text*?

	true	false	not in the text
1. Nobody lived in New York when Europeans went there.	☐	☐	☐
2. New York stayed capital of the USA for centuries.	☐	☐	☐
3. Immigrants often left their own countries because they could not live there.	☐	☐	☐
4. The first immigrant in New York was a girl from Ireland.	☐	☐	☐
5. The Statue of Liberty is on Ellis Island.	☐	☐	☐
6. Immigration to New York still goes on today.	☐	☐	☐

4 Korrigiere die Sätze aus Übung 3, die du mit *false* gekennzeichnet hast.

______

______

5 Vervollständige die folgenden Sätze mit Informationen aus dem Text.

1. The English ______ the Dutch in 1664, ______ New Amsterdam and then ______ ıt New York.
2. Immigrants ______ in Manhattan ______ the immigration station on Ellis Island was opened.
3. The number of people in New York ______ 1700 until 1898.
4. Immigrants have moved to New York ______ almost 400 years.

Listening: In a diner 6

6 Höre dir die beiden Dialoge an und beantworte die Fragen dazu.

1. What does the man order? ______________________

____

2. How much does it cost? ______________________

3. What is a special breakfast? ______________________

____

4. What does the woman order? ______________________

5. How much does it cost? ______________________

Writing: A postcard

7 Schau dir Dans Notizen an, dann formuliere daraus eine Postkarte an seine Mutter.

Dear Mum, ______________________ ______________________ ______________________ ______________________ ______________________ ______________________ ______________________ ______________________	arrived Thursday – found great hostel in Greenwich Village: still staying there – met some great guys: visited Chinatown and Empire State Building with them – sit in Central Park today and watched people – great

Speaking

8 Was könntest du in den folgenden Situationen sagen? Überlege.

1. You are visiting New York and your mum asks if you like it there.

____

2. You are going to visit the Statue of Liberty tomorrow. Your mum asks how you feel about it. You are excited about it.

____

3. You go to the top of the Empire State Building. You are very surprised at the great view.

____

4. Somebody tells you that their uncle died in the World Trade Centre.

____

Mediation

9 Du bist mit deiner Oma in New York. Sie will mit dir essen gehen. Hilf ihr bei der Kommunikation mit einem Einheimischen.

Oma: Frag ihn, ob es irgendwo hier in der Gegend etwas Gutes zu essen gibt.

Du: ____

Mann: Yes, there's a great diner around the corner. It sells delicious bagels.

Du: ____

Oma: Schön. Frag ihn noch, ob man leicht zum Zentrum kommt.

Du: ____

Mann: Well, downtown Manhattan isn't far. You can walk or take the subway.

Du: ____

Unit 2

People

1 Finde die sieben Wörter im Buchstabengitter, die in die Sätze gehören.

1. Students sometimes have to see the ____________.
2. He isn't a child, he's an ____________.
3. Nicola isn't a guy, she's a ____________.
4. Who's the ____________ of that book?
5. Who's Kyle? Is he that cool ____________ over there?
6. Are you a ____________ but not yet 18? Do you want a job?

e	a	u	t	d	u	d	e	a
f	c	q	e	z	j	i	s	d
h	t	a	e	n	g	u	x	u
p	r	i	n	c	i	p	a	l
b	o	k	s	y	r	d	p	t
n	n	e	a	m	l	o	c	k
l	s	c	a	u	t	h	o	r

School in the US

2 Vervollständige den folgenden Text mit den fehlenden Wörtern.

Hi. So you wanted to know about my school here in New York State? Well! We have eight p____________ a day and the first one usually starts at 8.30. If you are late for school or for c____________, you get d____________ after school. We have three s____________ every year. I'm in the 8th g____________ and I love it. And why? Because I'm a cheerleader now and so I can do extra g____________ every week and choose a boyfriend from the football team!

Politics

3 Löse die Anagramme auf und ergänze die Lücken.

aaadventg – tagsadvandie – scussidions – slaw – stopin – slipotic – actionsfiquail

If you want to go into ______________, you must enjoy debating important subjects. You don't need any special ______________ but you must know and care about the ______________ in your country. It is an ______________ if you can talk well because you must be able to convince people that your ideas are good. You need to be able to present your arguments well and be able to explain all the important ______________ both for and against. You have to enjoy ______________ and you will have a big ______________ if you cannot listen to people.

Verben

4 Übersetze die hervorgehobenen Verben.

1. Shall we check out that new shop? ______________
2. We need to elect a new student council. ______________
3. Oh no. I missed the training yesterday. ______________
4. John presented his ideas well, didn't he? ______________
5. He cheated in his exams. ______________
6. I need to practice those new dances. ______________
7. The thief grabbed my bag. ______________

Wichtige Wendungen

5 Setze die Satzteile zusammen, um Wendungen zu erhalten, die man bei einer Diskussion verwenden kann, und ordne sie richtig zu.

That's	I	I see what	As you	It's	I think
you're	you mean,	true,	obvious	agree	can
right.	see, …	with you.	but …	that …	but …

To present arguments: ______________________________

To agree: ______________________________

To disagree: ______________________________

6 Lieber britischer oder amerikanischer Fußball? Setze die Verbindungswörter an den richtigen Stellen ein.

because – but – but – finally – first – for example – next – so – that is why

I think we should play more soccer in the US and less football. And why? ____________, I think soccer is more important ____________ it is played all over the world. Every four years the football world championship is played with countries from all over the world. We play, too, ____________ the US never does well. ____________, sport is important in the US, ____________ most sports which we play are only played in a few countries, ____________ we usually win. ____________, baseball and American football are not played in many other countries at all. I think when more people play a sport, the level at which the sport is played gets higher. ____________ I think we should play a world sport like soccer in the US and not just an American sport. ____________, I think soccer is much more fun.

British English – American English

7 Wie lauten die folgenden Wörter in amerikanischem Englisch? Ändere das Wort oder die Schreibweise.

British	American	British	American
autumn	→ ______	lesson	→ ______
class/year	→ ______	mobile	→ ______
colour	→ ______	Mum	→ ______
favourite	→ ______	to organise	→ ______
jewellery	→ ______	to practise	→ ______

Adjektive

8 Löse die Adjektive aus der Wortschlange heraus und ordne sie dem ähnlichen Wort zu.

angry	______
last	______
clear	______
not open	______
great	______
tasty	______

Tipp Wenn du neue Wörter lernst, präge dir nicht nur die deutsche Übersetzung ein, sondern überlege, ob du bereits ein ähnliches Wort auf Englisch kennst oder die Vokabel auf Englisch erklären könntest.

Modale Hilfsverben mit dem Infinitiv Perfekt

Zu den modalen Hilfsverben gehören u. a. *must, should, can* und *could*. Man verwendet sie immer mit einem Infinitiv ohne *to:*

I **should** do my homework every day.

Wenn du sagen willst, dass etwas in der Vergangenheit hätte passieren können, sollen oder müssen, verwendest du die **Modalverben** mit dem **Infinitiv Perfekt:**

I **should have done** my homework yesterday. – Ich hätte meine Hausaufgaben gestern machen sollen.

He **must have worked** hard at school. – Er muss in der Schule hart gearbeitet haben.

We **might have won** if we had practiced more. – Wir hätten vielleicht gewonnen, wenn wir mehr trainiert hätten.

She **needn't have called** him. – Sie hätte ihn nicht rufen müssen.

They **could have asked** me to their party. – Sie hätten mich zu ihrer Party einladen können.

Die Perfektform des Infinitivs bildest du mit ***have*** + ***past participle.***

9 Formuliere aus den Satzteilen ganze Sätze mit Modalverb + Infinitiv Perfekt.

1. Neil and Billy – might – meet – in town – by chance

2. They – must – have a good time – at the diner

3. Neil – can't – split up – from his girlfriend

4. So – he – shouldn't – ask – Billy – to the dance

10 Beim Tanzen. Gib die Sätze mit einem Modalverb wieder.

1. Did Chan enjoy the dance? I don't know. It's possible.

(might) _ _ _______ enjoyed the dance.

2. I'm sure he liked me. He asked me, didn't he?

(must) _ _______ or he wouldn't have asked me.

3. I talked to Kate too much. Chan was probably bored.

(shouldn't) _ _______ to Kate so much.

4. I didn't dance with Chan very much.

(could) _ _______ with Chan more.

5. Why did I worry about another date? He's just asked me.

(needn't) _ _______ another date.

11 *Cheerleader try-outs:* Übersetze die Sätze ins Englische.

1. Die Aufnahmetests müssen früh gestartet haben.

. I .n sure I wasn't late.

2. Ich hätte vorher mehr üben sollen.

____

3. Sie hätte mir eine zweite Chance geben können.

____

4. Ich hätte überhaupt nicht hinzugehen brauchen.

____

Der Infinitiv des Passivs ohne *to*

Der Infinitiv Passiv wird aus ***be + past participle*** gebildet.

Der **Infinitiv Passiv ohne *to*** wird nach *will* verwendet, um die *will future*-Form des Passivs auszudrücken:

The cheerleaders **will be told** about their matches tomorrow. – Die Cheerleader werden morgen über ihre Spiele informiert werden.

Der Infinitiv Passiv ohne *to* wird auch nach modalen Hilfsverben verwendet:

Cheerleaders' photos **can be taken** many times at matches. – Fotos von den Cheerleadern können … gemacht werden.

Parents **must be asked** before students **can be offered** jobs. – Eltern müssen gefragt werden, bevor den Schülern Jobs angeboten werden können.

Das einzige modale Hilfsverb, das mit Passiv Infinitiv + *to* verwendet wird, ist *ought to*:

Teachers **ought to be asked,** too. – Die Lehrer sollten auch informiert werden.

12 *Our school rules.* Lies den Text und vervollständige die Lücken mit der korrekten Kombination von modalem Hilfsverb und Infinitiv Passiv.

We don't have a school uniform, but blue pullovers, trousers and skirts ____________ (must + wear). Dresses ____________ (can + wear), too. Mobile phones ____________ (may + take) to school but they ____________ (must not + use) in school. MP3 players ____________ (cannot + take) to school because they are not needed. Sandwiches ____________ (needn't + take) to school because school dinners ____________ (can + buy) in the cafeteria. If you are ill, a note ____________ (must + bring) from your parents.

Der Infinitiv des Passivs mit *to*

Der **Infinitiv Passiv mit *to*** wird verwendet nach Verben wie *hope, would like, want, expect, seem* oder *hate:*

I'd like **to be invited** to the party. – Ich würde gern zu der Party eingeladen werden.

She hopes **to be offered** a job. – Sie hofft, dass ihr ein Job angeboten wird.

They expect **to be informed.** – Sie erwarten informiert zu werden.

Wenn man sagen will, wer die Handlung verursacht hat, verwendet man den ***by-agent:***

I want **to be invited** to the dance **by** Alan. – Ich will von Alan zu dem Ball eingeladen werden.

13 *Young people today.* Übersetze die Sätze ins Englische.

1. Junge Menschen erwarten, dass ihnen gute Stellen gegeben werden, ohne dass sie arbeiten müssen.

_ without working.

2. Sie wollen bezahlt werden, auch wenn sie nicht arbeiten.

___ even when they don't work.

3. Sie hoffen, dass man sie in dämlichen Fernsehsendungen entdeckt.

_ in stupid television programmes.

4. Mein Enkel sagt, junge Menschen würden gern von uns alten Leuten verstanden werden.

My grandson says young _

by us old folk.

14 *At our school.* Gib die folgenden Sätze wieder, indem du sie mit dem Passiv umschreibst. Wenn passend, verwende den *by-agent*.

1. Teachers want people to treat them with respect.

____

2. Students expect teachers to teach them well.

____

3. People can leave bikes in the sheds.

____

4. Students must wear school uniforms.

____

5. Parents would like the teachers to inform them about their kids.

____

15 *Tips for going to a ball.* Verwende die vorgegebenen Wörter, um die Lücken mit dem Passiv zu vervollständigen.

Girls! So you ______________________ (want + invite) to the ball? Wake up! We're living in the 21st century – now boys ______________________ (can + ask) by you. But first a boy ______________________ (must + find). And first you must decide what you want. Do you want to dance at the ball? If you are lucky, good dancers ______________________ (may + find) at a dancing lesson. What? You just want a cool dude? Sorry! It ______________________ (has to + say): they aren't easy to find! Boys! So you ______________________ (expect + ask) to the ball by a 21st century girl? Dream on! Good luck ______________________ (must + create) first.

Lesen: *Pro and con texts*

16 Lies die Textabschnitte. Dann stelle sie in die richtige Reihenfolge, indem du ihnen die Überschriften zuordnest.

1. introduction _____
2. first argument for _____
3. second argument for _____
4. first argument against _____
5. second argument against _____
6. conclusion _____

A. One of the main arguments against school uniform is the price. If parents have to buy the school uniforms from one firm or even one shop, the uniforms are often expensive. The school might try to choose cheaper clothes, but if firms only make a small number of trousers, for example, they are always more expensive than if they make a large number. Even if pupils just have to wear any black trousers or blue pullovers, parents still have to buy more clothes all together: their children need uniforms as well as clothes for the weekend and the evening. At times when their children are growing fast, this can mean that parents have to buy two school uniforms in a year and two lots of normal clothes, too.

B. The main advantage of school uniform is that pupils can just go to school and do not feel as though they are going to a fashion show. In schools without uniform pupils are often made fun of because of their clothes. Other pupils laugh at them if their clothes are not trendy or if they are from a cheap shop. So they always feel under pressure to wear cool clothes. This is a big problem if they are not really interested in clothes or if their parents do not have enough money to buy them new or expensive things to wear. Pupils who have to wear a school uniform also do not have to think about what to put on in the morning.

C. When pupils wear school uniforms, everybody knows right away which school they go to. This is good for teachers if the pupils go on a school trip because they can always see who they have to look after out of school. Some people say that it is good for the pupils, too, because they feel they are a part of the school and that they need to work together and help each other. The idea is that when pupils wear school uniforms they cannot see their differences as easily, especially how rich their parents are.

D. Sometimes something that seems to be an advantage can actually be a disadvantage. For example, it can be an advantage when pupils all feel that they are part of a group, but when two groups of pupils from different schools meet each other, it can become a disadvantage. There might be fights because the pupils belong to two different groups. Clothes can also change how people feel. Pupils who have worn school uniforms since they were eleven or even seven often feel that uniforms are for children. When they grow older, they still feel or act like children if they have to wear a uniform. If they are allowed to wear normal clothes, they often feel and act more like adults.

E. In my opinion there are more disadvantages of school uniform than advantages. Although some people believe that when pupils wear school uniforms you cannot see how rich their parents are, this is not true. Even if pupils have to wear exactly the same clothes, they still have different shoes, coats or hair styles. People always find ways to show their differences. I think pupils should learn to respect each other's differences at school and not learn how to hide them.

F. In some countries, for example the UK and China, pupils have to wear school uniforms. Teachers, parents and even pupils in our country often say that we should have a school uniform, too, but what are the advantages and disadvantages. First of all we need to ask, what is a school uniform? A school uniform is the clothes which girls and boys have to wear at school. There are two main types of school uniform. In some schools pupils have to wear any kind of black trousers, a white shirt and a black pullover. In other schools the pupils have to wear a special type of black trousers and black pullover and the parents have to buy these from a special shop. And in some schools girls have to – or are allowed to – wear different things than boys. For example, girls might have to wear skirts and boys might have to wear jackets. There are different advantages and disadvantages for both types of uniforms.

17 Welche der Uniformen sind im Text erwähnt?

a) ☐

b) ☐

c) ☐

d) ☐

18 Lies den Text nochmals genau durch, dann beschäftige dich mit den folgenden Behauptungen. Sind sie nach Meinung des Autors *true* oder *false?* Korrigiere die falschen Sätze.

	true	false
1. You always have to buy school uniforms from the same shop.	☐	☐
2. School uniforms are always expensive.	☐	☐
3. Advantage: Pupils needn't wear trendy clothes.	☐	☐
4. Advantage: More difficult to see how rich the parents are.	☐	☐
5. Disadvantage: Teachers can see which school pupils go to from the uniform.	☐	☐
6. Disadvantage: Pupils act differently in a uniform.	☐	☐
7. School uniforms shouldn't be worn.	☐	☐
8. Differences should be hidden.	☐	☐

Korrektur:

19 In welchen Zeilen findest du diese Informationen?

1. It is more expensive to make a small number of things than a large number.

→ Z. _

2. Sometimes two school uniforms per year must be bought.

→ Z. _

3. Differences ought to be respected.

→ Z. _

Lesen und Schreiben: *Pro and con texts*

20 Lies den Text, dann wähle die beste Überschrift dafür aus.

A new football field ☐ A new friend ☐

A new sports hall ☐ A new job ☐

I'm not a great fan of meetings. I don't like listening to other people talking about things that don't interest me. That was why I arrived late at the student council school meeting. I know you should never be late for meetings, but I really shouldn't have been late this time. Somebody had put my name in the hat. When I arrived, I found out that I was now on the student council. Lots of people had voted for me. It must have been my enemies. It cannot have been my friends.

I walked into the hall and heard them read out my name. Everybody clapped and some people laughed. I tried to tell everybody that it was a mistake and that I didn't want to be on the student council, but nobody heard me. When my friend Brad saw me, he told me that I was too late and that I had to be on the council now. He said that it was great because I could try to get a new football field and seating area. He said I would be really good. I asked him if he had put my name in the hat and he said he would never do that to a friend. I think I might just have lost a friend!

The first student council meeting was on Wednesday evening after school. We met in a pizzeria. The old student council members organised it so that the new council members would come, too. It worked – I love pizzas. The problem was that I also had some homework to do for Friday, and on Thursday evening I had football practice. There were ten people in the school council and half of them were guys. I didn't know the others very well at first; they were from other grades.

By the end of the evening I knew them quite well and I had enjoyed myself. We ate and laughed and had a good time. They were all cool – well, apart from this one girl. She was not happy.

"I've got lots of homework to do," said Kate. "I don't have time to sit here and eat. I thought we were going to talk about something important."

One of the older guys calmly explained that it was usually easier to work together if you knew each other better and that you could work and have fun, but Kate was not convinced.

On Friday I got into trouble because I hadn't done my homework, so on Saturday I couldn't go and watch the match. I had to stay at home and do homework. Two weeks after the first meeting, we had the second one. I had homework again and really didn't want to go, but this time we wanted to talk about the new football pitch, so I went anyway. But first let me explain about the football pitch.

Our school is good at football. We won the schools' competition last year, and lots of people always come and watch us. There are so many people who come that we haven't got enough seats for them and we want to build some more. That's expensive and the school doesn't have enough money, so we need to raise money. The problem is that some people at school think we should raise money for other things!

We had the second meeting in a burger bar. Kate was not happy and typically she was also against the new football pitch and seating area. Kate said we needed a new gym for wheelchair sport. We have a few students in wheelchairs at our school. Although it's normal, it's more difficult to discuss some things with them. Obviously lots more people are interested in football than in wheelchair sport, but then there are fewer people in wheelchairs, so does that mean they should never get anything they want or need? People who can walk have an easier time. But does that mean we shouldn't try to get what we want?

We talked for hours and tried to decide what we should raise money for first. In the end my arguments won and we voted for the football pitch. It was great. A success! Next year we would have a new football pitch and I had helped to do this. I had even enjoyed it. It was a good feeling! I could convince people with my arguments. But I felt bad about Kate. I looked at her and she looked at me – angrily, I thought.

The next week I saw her when I got on the bus. She was going into town. I was embarrassed. I didn't know whether to say hello or not. At that moment she looked up and smiled, so I walked over and sat next to her. She didn't seem angry at all. She was happy and friendly, so I asked her if she minded about the new gym.

She laughed and said, "You know, you win some, you lose some. Why should I mind?"

We both got off the bus at the same place, and we discovered we were both going to the sport's shop. I wanted some new football boots and she needed new sports clothes. We went into the shop together and then she stopped. She couldn't get any farther into the shop. There wasn't enough room for her wheelchair. I was surprised and angry. "Why don't they leave more room?" I asked.

"Oh, they just don't think," she answered.

"Doesn't it make you angry?" I asked.

"Chuck, I've been in a wheelchair all my life. If I got angry every time I couldn't do something, I wouldn't enjoy life at all."

I enjoyed talking to Kate and when she told me she was going to basketball training the next day, I asked if I could go and watch. She laughed and said I could go and play if I wanted. So I did. Wheelchair basketball was great to watch, and, as I found out when I tried to play, it is also very difficult. We went out for a pizza that evening and I told her how she seemed so angry at the student council meeting and how I had thought she must be no fun

at all. She explained that she hadn't really wanted to be on the student council. She didn't have enough time. She played wheelchair basketball three times a week and she did other sport. She said she needed it to keep her body fit, and she worked hard because she wanted to be a reporter when she left school.
"And, you know, there aren't many reporters in wheelchairs. It is possible, but I need to be better than everybody else if I want to do it," she explained.
After that we often met. We had fun together and I found out that life was about more than just football and school.

21 Lies die Fragen zum Text und notiere die richtigen Antworten – es können auch mehrere sein.

1. Chuck doesn't like meetings because …
a) he doesn't like listening to people talk about boring things.
b) he doesn't like talking about boring things.
c) he never likes listening to people talk. → ____ ____

2. Which of these sentences are true?
a) Chuck didn't want to be in the student council.
b) He liked all the other people in the council.
c) He enjoyed the meetings. → ____ ____

3. They needed a new football pitch …
a) so that people in wheelchairs could use it.
b) so that more people could go and watch.
c) so that they could play football better. → ________

4. Kate …
a) didn't like Chuck at first.
b) was angry that they didn't want a new sports hall.
c) didn't want to go to a meeting because she didn't have enough time. → ________

5. In the end …
a) Chuck tried to play wheelchair basketball.
b) Kate and Chuck became friends.
c) the school got a new sports hall, too. → ________

22 Lies die folgenden Aussagen. Sind es Vorteile oder Nachteile, im *student council* zu sein, oder haben sie gar nichts mit dem *student council* zu tun? Notiere *advantage, disadvantage* oder *not important* neben den Sätzen.

1. Student council meetings take lots of time. ____
2. Wheelchair basketball is not so popular. ____
3. You can change things at school. ____
4. You can make new friends there. ____
5. You find out new things. ____
6. Meetings can be boring. ____
7. You can have fun. ____
8. You can learn to be a reporter. ____

23 Verfasse einen kurzen Text darüber, ob es gut oder schlecht ist, im *student council* zu sein. Verwende dazu Wendungen und Vokabeln aus Übung 16.

Hörverstehen: *Discussions*

Sich vorbereiten
Sammle vor einer Diskussion Informationen und überlege: Welche Argumente willst du vorbringen? Welche Gegenargumente könnten gebracht werden? Bereite mögliche Antworten vor.

Argumente präsentieren
Überlege, welche Wendungen nützlich sein könnten, um deine Argumente vorzubringen oder um jemandem (nicht) zuzustimmen.

Diskutieren üben
Diskutieren kann man lernen. Bleibe immer höflich und überlege nach der Diskussion, was gut gelaufen ist und was nicht. Was könntest du beim nächsten Mal besser machen?

Zuhören: *MP3 players in schools 1* 7

24 Überlege dir zunächst Argumente dafür und dagegen, ob MP3-Player in der Schule erlaubt sein sollten. Dann höre dir die Diskussion von Jed und Jill mit zwei Lehrern an. Welche Argumente werden vorgebracht?

Arguments **for** MP3 players in school:

1. ____________________

2. ____________________

3. ____________________

4. ____________________

Arguments **against** MP3 players in school:

1. ____________________

2. ____________________

3. ____________________

4. ____________________

5. ____________________

25 Mit welchen Wendungen kann man gut Argumente vorbringen und Zustimmung oder Ablehnung äußern? Höre dir CD-Track 7 nochmals an. Welche Ausdrücke werden verwendet?

To present arguments: ______________________________

____

To agree: ______________________________

____

To disagree: ______________________________

____

26 Nochmal CD-Track 7: Beantworte die folgenden Fragen.

1. What do they have problems with at school? ____________
2. What other things do students talk about? ____________
3. When are they going to talk about MP3 players again? ____________

   ____
4. What does Mr Elliot teach? ____________

Zuhören und sprechen: *MP3 players in schools 2* 8

27 Höre dir die Diskussion nochmals an. Jetzt sind jeweils Pausen gelassen, in denen du selbst zustimmen und ablehnen sollst.

1. Agree with Jill.
2. Disagree with the teacher.
3. Agree with the teacher.
4. Disagree with the teacher.
5. Agree with Jill.

Unit 3

Pictures

1 Sieh dir die Bilder an und beschrifte sie.

1.

a) ______________

b) ______________

2.

a) ______________

b) ______________

c) ______________

Abstrakte Substantive: *Word formation*

2 *At the Grand Canyon.* Leite aus den Wörtern die korrekten Substantive ab.

natural: The Grand Canyon was formed by __________.

real: There are great photos of it, but none of them come near to __________.

beautiful: You can see the whole __________ of the area from the Skywalk.

explain: It's difficult to believe the __________ of how the canyon was formed.

like: It doesn't matter what your __________ and dislikes are, you'll love it here.

People and places

3 Kreuzworträtsel. Löse es und stelle das Lösungswort aus den hinterlegten Buchstaben zusammen.

1. a part of town outside downtown
2. a boyfriend and girlfriend or man and wife
3. some land on which the first people who lived in America can now live
4. a person who helped found a village or town
5. a person who is one of a group, a team or a club
6. the land of area around us
7. a group of families who live together
8. a part of the US – there are 50 of them
9. a person who writes for a newspaper

A person who lived in the US before white people arrived: ______________

4 *Odd one out.* Finde das Wort, das nicht in die Reihe passt.

1.	2.	3.	4.
Mexican	French	the French	dude
Mexico	Mexican	the English	tribe
American	English	the American	guys
Indian	Scot	the Mexicans	couple
→ ______	→ ______	→ ______	→ ______

Verben

5 Übersetze die folgenden Verben.

to keep	______________	to admire	______________
to point	______________	to portray	______________
to mix	______________	to experience	______________
to develop	______________		

6 *Skiing.* Ergänze die fehlenden Präpositionen.

I've always dreamt ________ going skiing, but I never thought I'd be able to because it's so expensive. When two friends started talking ________ a skiing holiday, I let them talk. They'd often organised things and I'd got excited but then they'd let me ________. But then they said there was a school trip to the slopes. "Come ________ to the meeting," they said.

I went. I was afraid ________ it being very expensive and it was, but this time I really felt ________ a holiday, so I decided to get a job and pay for myself. I looked ________ a job and found one. I looked forward ________ the skiing holiday all winter but even when I got ________ the bus to the mountains in February, I couldn't believe that I was really going. We got there and I loved it. I wasn't good ________ skiing but I loved the beautiful environment, and I think even if I lived there, I'd never get tired ________ the beautiful views and the snow.

Adjektive

7 Löse die Anagramme auf und setze die Adjektive richtig ein.

kinghatbrate **ghue** **wlo** **thicalmy** **lantura**

axeldre **oiusser** **singprisur** **gluy**

I'm not joking. I'm ______________.

That's a ______________ bridge, isn't it? Can big ships go under there?

Is the Loch Ness Monster real? Or is it a ______________ animal?

I didn't expect that at all. That's very ______________.

The view is amazing. It's ______________.

The Grand Canyon is ______________. People didn't make it.

The Grand Canyon is very long. It's ______________.

She's always ______________. Nothing much worries her at all.

Tastes are different. What one person thinks is beautiful, the other thinks is

______________.

American English vs. British English

8 Wie ändert sich die Schreibung dieser englischen Vokabeln? Oder musst du ein ganz anderes Wort verwenden?

to practise	______________	trousers	______________
travelling	______________	railway	______________
motorway	______________	jewellery	______________

Wichtige Wendungen: *Small talk / being positive*

9 Verbinde die Satzteile miteinander, um sinnvolle Sätze zu bilden.

1. Excuse me for asking,	the slopes.
2. Would you recommend	but I don't agree.
3. I just love hitting	seeing the Skywalk?
4. The people here	no problem.
5. You're right	but are you from Texas?
6. Excuse me, could you	about that.
7. Have a	are very nice.
8. I'm sorry,	great vacation!
9. Nice to	spaces here are fantastic.
10. I'd be happy to,	meet you.
11. The open	to have met you.
12. It was really nice	take a picture of us, please?

10 Ordne die Wendungen aus Übung 9 den passenden Gelegenheiten zu.

Starting a conversation: ____________________

Continuing a conversation: ____________________

Finishing a conversation: ____________________

Disagreeing: ____________________

Agreeing: ____________________

Replying to a question: ____________________

Bedingungssätze (Wiederholung)

Bedingungssätze sind Sätze mit *if*. Es gibt drei Arten:

Typ 1: Etwas könnte passieren, muss aber nicht:

If it **snows, I'll go** skiing tomorrow. – Falls es schneit, gehe ich morgen Ski fahren (es könnte schneien oder auch nicht).

Typ 2: Etwas ist unwahrscheinlich oder unmöglich:

If I **won** 200 dollars, I **would go** skiing. – Wenn ich 200 Dollar gewinnen würde, würde ich Ski fahren gehen (aber ich gewinne sie wohl eher nicht).

Typ 3: Es war etwas in der Vergangenheit unwahrscheinlich oder unmöglich:

If I **hadn't gone** skiing, I **wouldn't have broken** my leg. – Wenn ich nicht Ski fahren gegangen wäre, hätte ich mir nicht das Bein gebrochen (ich habe es mir aber gebrochen).

11 *My own car*. Trage die richtige Zeitform in die Lücken ein.

I'd visit my friend in the mountains and go skiing this weekend if I __________ (have) a car. I don't have much money. If I __________ (have) enough money, I __________ (buy) a car. I'm looking for a job. If I __________ (find) one, I __________ (buy) my own car in a few months. If I __________ (not/find) a job quickly, I __________ (not/can) go skiing this winter again. But I'm lucky: if I __________ (not/get) my driver's license last June, I __________ (not/can) go skiing last month. But then if I __________ (not/have) an accident in my mum's car, she __________ (lend) me hers.

Das *gerund* als Subjekt und Objekt des Satzes

Das ***gerund*** ist eine Form des Verbs, die wie ein Nomen verwendet wird. Man bildet es wie das *present participle* aus Infinitiv + *-ing*. Es gelten dieselben Schreibregeln:

ski → skiing; stop → stopping; write → writing

Wie ein Nomen kann das *gerund* **Subjekt** eines Satzes sein. Dabei kann es
- allein stehen: **Skiing** is my favourite hobby.
- mit einem Nomen: **Watching TV** is boring.
- mit einer adverbialen Bestimmung: **Working in a diner** can be fun.

Wie ein Nomen kann das *gerund* auch **Objekt** eines Satzes sein:
- nach Verben, die eine Vorliebe oder eine Abneigung ausdrücken, z. B. *to enjoy, to love, to hate, can't stand, don't mind:* I **love relaxing** in front of the TV.
- nach anderen Verben wie z. *B. finish, stop, start, imagine, keep, risk:* Please **stop doing** that. I can't **imagine working** every day.

Nach *love, like, hate* und *start* kann auch der Infinitiv mit *to* verwendet werden. Es gibt keinen Bedeutungsunterschied:
In the afternoon it **started raining** = In the afternoon it **started to rain.**

12 *Last weekend.* Lies den Text und unterstreiche die *gerunds*.

I love lying in bed and getting up late at the weekend, so last weekend when the phone rang at 10 am, I was still lying in bed. It was a new friend. She wanted to know if I liked skiing and if I wanted to go to the mountains with her. I lay there and imagined skiing down a mountain. It was beautiful. Listening to great music in a car while you are driving through beautiful countryside is wonderful, too. I wanted to go but an hour later she was sitting in her car and driving to the Rockies and I was still lying in bed. I can't ski! I'm going to start learning. Tomorrow!

13 In Montana. Formuliere anhand der Satzteile vollständige Sätze mit dem *gerund.*

1. I – to love – to live – in Montana

2. Tomorrow – I – going to start – to learn – to ride – a horse

3. I – can – to imagine – to go – to school – on – my horse

4. To drive – a car – to be – boring

14 *Moving house.* Übersetze die folgenden Sätze und verwende dabei *gerunds.*

1. Ich hatte mir schon oft vorgestellt, in Kalifornien zu wohnen.

2. Ich schwimme sehr gern im Meer und surfe.

3. Es ist nicht sehr spannend, in Kansas zu leben.

4. Ich dachte nicht, dass es mir etwas ausmachen würde umzuziehen.

5. Aber es ist viel schwieriger als erwartet, deine Freunde zurückzulassen.

Das *gerund* nach Präpositionen

Das ***gerund*** kann wie ein Nomen nach Präpositionen verwendet werden. Es kann ***nach Verb + Präposition*** stehen:

	Verb + Präposition	*gerund*	
I	dreamt of	living	in California.
John	feels like	going	home.
He	talks about	seeing	his friends.

Weitere Verben + Präposition, auf die ein *gerund* folgt, sind z. B. *to care about, to think of, to look forward to.*

Ebenso kann das *gerund* **nach Adjektiv + Präposition** stehen:

	Adjektiv + Präposition	*gerund*	
I'm	good at	speaking	Spanish.
Are you	interested in	going	to the cinema?
He is	afraid of	driving	in the snow.

Weitere Adjektive + Präposition, auf die ein *gerund* folgt, sind z. B. *to be bad at, to be tired of, to get used to, to be worried about, to be famous for.*

Bei *to look forward to* and *to get used to* ist das zweite *to* eine Präposition: I've got used **to** getting up early.

15 *Vacation.* Bilde Sätze in der richtigen Wortreihenfolge.

1. forward – looking – are – doing – what – holidays – you – your – to – in – ?

___

2. talking – visiting – about – are – we – California

___

3. I – Route 66 – driving – interested – am – in – along

___

4. about – are – bored – car – getting – in – the – we – worried

___

16 In den *Rockies.* Unterstreiche die *gerunds.*

I've always dreamt of going to the Rockies. I've imagined walking through the mountains and sleeping under the clear sky. I've always been crazy about watching animals in their own environment. Now my dream has come true and it's as beautiful and exciting as I imagined. Now I'm sitting by a river and watching fish jump out. Wild cats are watching them, too. It's great and I could stay here forever. I'm not looking forward to going home back to my city life again.

17 *Sport.* Finde die Fehler im Text, streiche sie durch und korrigiere sie rechts.

My children keep telling me I should doing more sport but ____________
it's more difficult than they think. I don't like jog and I can't ____________
get used to go to the gym. I love to cycle, but the last time ____________
I was rideing my bike into town, a car almost hit me. I love ____________
skiing but obviously you can only doing that in winter. One ____________
of my favorite hobbies is swiming in the sea but we live in ____________
Texas so I can't do that very often. I stopped do gymnastics ____________
when I stopped being a cheerleader. I'd like trying in-line ____________
skating but I'm scared of break my leg. I'm very interested ____________
in rock climbing and I could practising on a climbing wall ____________
in the gym but I don't want to risk haveing an accident. I ____________
like football but I'm not very good at play with balls, so I'll ____________
just have to keep watching it on TV! ____________

Die Objekt + *-ing*-Form-Konstruktion

Du kannst über das Verhalten anderer reden, indem du ein Nomen oder Pronomen vor die *-ing*-Form-Konstruktion einfügst:

I love **my friends sending** text messages to me. – Ich finde es toll, wenn meine Freunde mir SMS schicken.

I'm looking forward to **my brother moving out** of our house. – Ich freue mich darauf, dass mein Bruder bei uns auszieht.

But I'm worried about **him not coming** home again. – Aber ich mache mir Sorgen, dass er nicht wieder nach Hause kommt.

Das Nomen oder Pronomen ist eigentlich das Objekt des Satzes, von der Bedeutung her ist es aber Subjekt der *-ing*-Form-Konstruktion: *My brother* ist Objekt von *looking forward to,* gleichzeitig aber derjenige (Subjekt), der auszieht.

Das Pronomen steht meist in der Objektform (me, him, them) kann aber auch, im förmlichen Stil, als Possessivbegleiter stehen (my, his, they):

I'm worried about **him/his** having an accident.

Im sehr förmlichen Stil kann auch der *s*-Genitiv verwendet werden:

She was used to her **mother's** helping her. – Sie war es gewöhnt, dass ihre Mutter ihr half.

18 *Thoughts on my family*. Bilder vollständige Sätze.

sister – my – my – I – am – wearing – tired – of – clothes.

____

arguing – like – don't – my – I – parents.

____

happy – they – about – fighting – aren't – too – us.

____

19 Nick erzählt von seinem Umzug nach Kalifornien. Notiere das Subjekt der *-ing*-Form-Konstruktion.

1. I wasn't crazy about my dad getting a job in California. his dad
2. I was afraid of my friends forgetting me. ____________
3. I'm a New Yorker and I'm not good at speaking clearly. ____________
4. At first I worried about Californians not understanding me. ____________
5. I'm bad at making new friends. ____________
6. I needn't have worried about my new classmates being friendly. ____________
7. I'm still looking forward to seeing my old friends again. ____________

20 Übersetze die folgenden Sätze von Shirley ins Englische.

1. Ich bin total begeistert davon, dass ich Cheerleaderin werde.

____

2. Ich mag es, wenn meine Freunde beim Training zuschauen.

____

3. Ich bin ein wenig nervös, dass ich bei einem Spiel einen Fehler machen könnte.

____

4. Ich mache mir Sorgen, dass mich die Fans auslachen könnten.

____

5. Ich freue mich darauf, mich mit einem Fußballspieler zu verabreden.

____

Das Passiv (Wiederholung)

Wenn du die Handlung betonen willst und nicht denjenigen, der für die Handlung verantwortlich ist, verwendest du das Passiv. Es steht oft in Zeitungsberichten oder historischen Texten.

Wenn du sagen willst, wer für etwas verantwortlich ist, verwendest du einen *by-agent:* I was invited **by Dick** to his party.

Das Passiv wird gebildet mit einer Form von ***to be + past participle.***

simple present	American football **is played** in America.
simple past	The Grand Canyon **was created** by a river.
present perfect	I **have** never **been interviewed** by a journalist.
past perfect	New Amsterdam **had been founded** by the Dutch before the English arrived.
will-future	**Will** the new road **be finished** soon?
infinitive	Your schoolwork should **be done** before you get a job.

Wenn du einen Aktivsatz in einen Passivsatz umwandeln willst, wird das Objekt des Aktivsatzes zum Subjekt des Passivsatzes.

21 *A new job.* Formuliere diese Sätze um, indem du sie ins Passiv verwandelst.

1. They hadn't advertised the job for long.

2. I had to ask my parents before we could agree everything.

3. They will open the museum tomorrow.

4. People often do not understand the Native American lifestyle very well.

5. Somebody has offered me a job in a new museum about Native Americans.

22 *Europeans and Native Americans.* Ergänze die richtigen Passiv- oder Aktivformen.

Native Americans ______________________ (not/always/treat) badly by Europeans since the two peoples met. When the first villages ________ __________________ (found) by white settlers, Native Americans and Europeans often __________________ (try) to talk to each other. Settlers were helped by the Americans when they ____________________ (have) problems to find enough food. Native Americans, of course, didn't need ______________________ (help) by the settlers. Later, as more and more Europeans ___________________ (arrive) and more and more land _____________________ (need), Native Americans __________________________ (push) off their land. If they did not go, they _______________________ (kill). Land that _____________________ (use) by the Americans for thousands of years was quickly taken from them. In the 19th century reservations ______________________ (create) for Native Americans. Native Americans _____________________ (have) any choice. Now Native Americans and their lifestyle ___________________________ (usually/respect) by Europeans. Native Americans must ______________ ___________ (treat) the same as all other Americans but, of course, their lifestyle ___________________________ (change) for ever. The land cannot ____________________ (use) as it once was.

Tipp Wenn du die Lücken vervollständigt hast, lies den Text nochmals durch. Hören sich die Sätze richtig an?

Die Verlaufsformen des Passivs

Neben den *simple forms* gibt es auch zwei *progressive forms* des Passivs. Sie werden gebildet mit einer Form des Verbs ***to be*** + ***being*** + ***past participle.***

Das ***present progressive*** wird verwendet, um über Sachen zu sprechen, die gerade ablaufen und nicht beendet sind:

A new road **is** just **being finished** in town (wird gerade fertiggestellt).

Some new subjects **are being taught** in school at the moment (werden gerade unterrichtet).

Signalwörter sind *just, at the moment, now.*

Das ***past progressive*** wird verwendet, um über Ereignisse zu reden, die zu einem bestimmten Zeitpunkt in der Vergangenheit passiert und nicht abgeschlossen waren:

What **was being repaired** when you arrived? – Was wurde (gerade) repariert, als du ankamst?

Our names **were being called** as we ran to the plane. – Unsere Namen wurden (gerade) aufgerufen, als wir zum Flugzeug rannten.

Signalwörter sind *when, while, as, during.*

23 *The Skywalk.* Bilde vollständige Sätze aus den Satzteilen mit den *progressive*-Formen des Passivs.

1. The Skywalk – to build – when – I – first – visit – the Grand Canyon

____

2. Lots of articles – to write – about it – at that time

____

3. Not – as many – negative articles – write – about it – now

____

24 Schau dir die Bilder an und vervollständige die Sätze.

1. ______________________________ (to open) when I arrived.

2. ______________________________ (to prepare).

3. ______________________________ (to lay) when I walked into the café.

4. ______________________________ (to serve) while I am reading my magazine.

25 *The burglar.* Muss das Passiv in der *progressive*- oder *simple*-Form stehen?

Some jewellery ____________________ (steal) at school on Monday and when I arrived yesterday questions ____________________ (ask) by the police. The burglar ________________________ (never/catch) but some of the things _________________________ (find) in a bird's nest a week later.

Das Passiv bei Verben mit Präpositionen

Verb und Präposition werden in englischen Passivsätzen nicht voneinander getrennt:

Subjekt (Aktiv)	Verb + Präposition	Objekt
The police	**is looking for**	*some jewellery which was stolen.*

Subject (Passiv)	Verb + Präposition	Objekt
Some jewellery which was stolen	**is being looked for**	by the police.

26 *The Grand Canyon.* Formuliere die folgenden Sätze neu, indem du sie mit dem Passiv bildest.

1. The Colorado River carved out the Grand Canyon.

____

2. Tribes of Native Americans lived on the land before Europeans moved there.

____

3. The National Park looks after the environment.

____

4. Developers have not built on the land much.

____

5. People have flown over and driven through the canyon.

____

6. Anybody who has seen it once must have dreamt about it.

____

Grammar skills

Grammatik verstehen
Grammatik ist sozusagen das versteckte Muster in einer Sprache. Als Kleinkind lernst du deine Muttersprache automatisch über dieses Muster. Wenn du in der Schule eine neue Sprache lernst, musst du dir ein neues Muster aneignen. Du durchschaust diese neue Grammatik am besten, wenn du ihre Regeln kennst und weißt, mit welchen Begriffen sie arbeitet. Beispielsweise gibt es im Deutschen kein *present progressive*, aber du hast gelernt, dass es im Englischen dazu verwendet wird, Dinge zu beschreiben, die gerade passieren.

Welcher Lerntyp bist du?
Eine Fremdsprache lernt man aber nicht nur, indem man die Grammatikregeln paukt. Auch durch Hören oder den Rhythmus der Vokabeln, Wendungen und ganzen Sätze kann man sich eine Sprache aneignen. Überlege, wie dir das Sprachenlernen am leichtesten fällt!

27 Sieh dir die Sätze an, dann überlege: Um welche Wortart handelt es sich bei den hervorgehobenen Wörtern (z. B. Substantiv, Pronomen, Adjektiv)? Welche Funktion haben sie (z. B. Subjekt, Objekt)? Dann bilde ähnliche Sätze, die für dich zutreffen, indem du die markierten Wörter austauschst.

1. (a) **I** have always been (b) **good** at **skiing** (c).

a) ____________________, b) ____________________, c) ____________________

____

2. My (a) **parents** are worried about (b) **my** not (c) **doing** well at school.

a) ____________________, b) ____________________, c) ____________________

____

3. (a) **Photos** were being (b) **taken** as I arrived (c) **on the slopes.**

a) ____________________, b) ____________________, c) ____________________

____

Lesen: *Love at first sight?*

28 Lies zunächst den Text, dann die voranstehenden Zusammenfassungen. Welche davon passt am besten?

a) Two stories are being told in "Love at first sight". The story of John and Ana has a happy ending. The chief is rescued and John and Ana fall in love. The ending of the real life story is not as happy.

b) Kyla is from the Hualapai tribe and Vince is a famous white American film star and he is playing the hero in the film. The film has a happy ending – they fall in love. The ending of the real life story is not yet clear.

c) Kyla is a Native American and she is playing the role of a Native American in a film. Vince is a famous white American film star and he is playing the hero in the film. They fall in love in the film and in real life.

→ Zusammenfassung ________ passt am besten.

John turned around and looked at the man behind him. The Native American chief (*Häuptling*) was tired. He had been shot and he would probably die, but he sat with his head held high on the horse. He must have been in pain, but John could not see any signs of it in his face.
"We'll be there soon," John said and he spoke in Navajo, but even as he said it he knew that he needn't have said anything. Chief, as John called him, knew the area much better than John did. John looked around. Monument Valley! It was the most beautiful place in the world for him and he wanted to stay there, but would he be able to? Would he ever be allowed to live with the Navajo people?
The sun was going down as John and Chief rode into the Navajo village. Some children saw them first and came running towards them. They called to their parents and their friends. They shouted and sang with happiness. John jumped down from his horse. He saw Ana, Chief's daughter, and her brothers coming out of their house. They walked to their father and helped him off his horse. Ana looked at John and then looked away. Her brothers said thank you and walked with their father into the house. The women of the village started cooking food. They were going to celebrate that night. John rode down to the river and jumped into the water. He swam and relaxed and thought about the last few days.
The Americans wanted the Navajo people to move to a reservation. They wanted the land for themselves, but although John was an American, he did not agree with their plans. He had too much respect for the Navajo. The Navajo did not want to go to a reservation and they had fought the Whites.

Chief had been hurt and then the American soldiers had taken him with them. They knew that the Navajo would not leave him there to die and they hoped to convince the Navajo to go to the reservation. But John had rescued him first. Now John would never be able to go back to his life as an American soldier.
John went back to the Indian village. They had already started celebrating. The children ran to him when they saw him. He played with them and threw them up in the air. Then he looked towards the fire. Chief was sitting in his usual place and Ana was sitting next to him. She looked up just at that moment. Was that a smile on her face? John was invited to sit with them. He sat between Chief and Ana. The chief's sons gave him some food and offered him the peace pipe.
John relaxed at last. He loved listening to the music and watching them dancing. He felt at home. He talked to Ana and they laughed. He was sure that Ana was allowed to be with him, he hoped he would be allowed to marry her. At the end of the evening they kissed.

"Cut!" shouted the director. "That was great. We'll finish there now. You can go back to the hotel. And don't forget the interview this evening."
Vince and Kyla got up and started walking to their changing rooms. Vince looked across at Kyla. She was so beautiful and so interesting, but he knew so little about her. She never wanted to talk to him. She always seemed angry and unhappy after they finished filming. Why? Why wouldn't she be friendly? Five minutes ago they had been kissing and now she wouldn't even look at him. How could she do that?

That evening John and Kyla had to do the interview in the hotel garden. It was their first interview.
"So what's it like working with Vince Redford, the world famous actor?" the journalist asked Kyla.
"Great," she said – and she sounded so serious that Vince looked at her quickly. "He's a great actor and I've learnt more than I ever imagined."
"And is Kyla the next young star?" the journalist asked Vince.
"Well. She's the best new actress I've ever worked with. She's very natural but ...," he paused. Here it was Kyla's turn to look at Vince. What was he going to say? She knew why she would never be a big cinema star. Did he?
"... she's from the Hualapai tribe. How many Native American stars do you know?" finished Vince.
Kyla looked at Vince again. He had surprised her. How did he know that she was from the Hualapai? Americans never knew or cared what tribe she was from. She was just a Native American. And did he really understand that Native Americans were still treated unfairly hundreds of years after the Europeans had arrived?
The journalist was still asking Vince questions but Kyla had stopped listen-

ing and started thinking. Maybe she had been unfair. She had thought she knew all about white Americans. She looked across at Vince. Maybe it was time to start being a bit fairer. It was time to start listening.
"And does the film have a happy ending?" the interviewer was now asking Vince as Kyla started listening again.
"Yes, of course," he smiled, "And in the best tradition of Hollywood cinema a white American is the hero."
Kyla looked at Vince again and this time she could not stop herself from smiling back again.
"And will the story of Vince and Kyla have a happy ending, too?" asked the journalist, who had noticed how they both kept looking at each other.
Vince looked over at Kyla and thought, maybe!

29 Verwende die folgenden Aussagen, um den Plot des Films sowie das *Making of* zu beschreiben. Die Sätze können für beides gelten.

They have an interview with a journalist.
She's a Native American and he's a white American.
The hero rescues him.
They film together but she doesn't talk to him.
She starts to understand the hero.
The American Government want the Navajo to move to a reservation.
She doesn't like the hero.
They fight and soldiers hurt and catch the chief.
At the end the hero and the woman kiss.

The story in the film:	The story of making the film:
______________________	______________________
______________________	______________________
______________________	______________________
______________________	______________________
______________________	______________________
______________________	______________________
______________________	______________________
______________________	______________________

30 In welcher/-n Zeile/-n kannst du folgende Informationen finden?

1. John could speak Navajo. ________
2. The Navajo lived in or near Monument Valley. ________
3. John wanted to live with the Navajo People. ________
4. The Navajo People made music and danced. ________
5. Vince wanted to get to know Kyla. ________
6. Kyla liked working with Vince. ________
7. Vince didn't think Kyla would be a world star. ________
8. Kyla hadn't been friendly to Vince because he was a white American. ________
9. The journalist thinks (or hopes) Kyla and Vince will fall in love. ________

31 Die folgenden Sätze umschreiben bestimmte Sätze im Text. Suche sie mit Angabe der Zeilen heraus und schreibe sie auf.

1. John was sure that something was hurting him.

____

2. It was sunset as John and Chief …

____

3. … and she was not joking.

____

4. … a smile danced on her face.

____

Zuhören und Schreiben: *Small talk* 9

32 Höre dir die drei Dialoge an, dann ordne sie jeweils einem Bild zu.

a)

b)

c)

d)

dialogue 1: ______, dialogue 2: ______, dialogue 3: ______

33 Höre die Gespräche nochmals an und beantworte die Fragen.

Dialogue 1:

1. Why is the man having a party? ____________________

2. How does the woman know he's having a party? ____________________

____

Dialogue 2:

1. Why did the woman say she was sorry? ____________________

2. Where's the man from? ____________________

3. Where has he been living for a year? ____________________

4. What does he like about the States? ______________________

____

Dialogue 3:

1. Where is the woman from? ______________________

2. What is she doing there? ______________________

3. When did she arrive? ______________________

4. What does the man recommend doing? ______________________

34 In welchem der drei Dialoge hörst du die folgenden Sätze? Höre sie dir nochmals an, trage die Ziffern ein und überprüfe deine Antworten.

Nice day today, isn't it? ________________

Wow. What a great view! ________________

Have a nice day. ________________

It was really nice to have met you. ________________

I just love an English accent. ________________

May I ask you where you're from? ________________

Excuse me for asking, but are you from England? ________________

Zuhören: *American or British?* 10

35 Höre dir an, wie diese Personen sprechen. Sind sie aus den USA oder aus England? Welche Vokabeln sind typisch für das jeweilige Land?

Man: ______________; words: ______________________________

Woman: ______________; words: ______________________________

Revision B (Unit 2–3)

Reading: Moving west

1 Lies den Text und ordne den Inhaltsbeschreibungen einen Absatz zu.

1. Sally's mum discovers Sally's dad's unhappy.
2. They talk about moving to Montana.
3. Sally's family enjoy themselves in Montana.
4. Sally's mum discovers Sally's unhappy.
5. They're about to move.
6. They travel to Montana.

1. _____ 2. _____ 3. _____ 4. _____ 5. _____ 6. _____

A. Sally walked into their flat and closed the door with a bang. Her mum was making dinner in the kitchen and thought, oh no, not again. Sally had not been so easy in the last few months. It's her age, thought her mum. Fifteen is a difficult age. Sally disappeared into her room and stayed there. Her mum left her alone.

B. At dinner Sally's mum could see that she had been crying. Her brother could see it, too. "What's up with you? Had an argument with Mick again?" Luke asked. Sally's mum, Sophie, looked up to see how Sally would react. Luke and Sally were always arguing and she expected Sally to shout at her brother. But she did not. She just looked at her plate and said that there was nothing wrong. At that moment Sally's dad walked in and the door closed behind him with a bang. Sophie thought, oh no, he must have had a bad day in the office – again.

C. "What's wrong, Henry?" she asked when he walked into the dining room. Henry didn't look good. He looked at his children and then at his wife. Sophie knew something must have happened. Had his firm closed? Henry had expected this to happen for some time. It wouldn't be the end of the world, thought Sophie. She had her job. They could survive till he found another job.
"The office is going to be closed down," said Henry. "I have to move to Montana."
There was silence around the table. Sally didn't look happy or unhappy.
"Montana! Great! I could have my own horse," Luke said excitedly.
"Do you want to go?" Sophie asked her husband.
"I don't know. I hoped the firm would make it. I hoped they would give us some

more time but now I don't know. The job would be good. We could have our own house. It'd be interesting to live in a different part of the States. But I don't want to take the children away from their friends and schools. And what about your job?"
"Well, I could work from home in Montana. What do you think, Sally?"
"I don't care. Montana, New York. What's the difference?"
"Maybe we should go and visit Montana. It's the school vacation next week. We could go and see what we think," said Sophie. She looked around the table, and everybody agreed, but Sally still didn't look her in the eyes. Oh God. Please don't let it be anything too terrible, thought Sophie.

D. A week later they arrived at a lodge in the mountains near Helena, the capital of Montana. It had taken them two days to drive there. Sally had hardly said a word, and now Sophie was sure it had something to do with her boyfriend, Mick. She hadn't phoned or sent text messages. She hadn't even phoned her best friend, Lisa. In fact she had left her cell phone at home. What was going on? At least Luke had been excited all the way and so the journey hadn't been so bad.

E. When they arrived at the lodge, they were welcomed by the owner and his family. They were very friendly and everybody felt at home quite quickly. It was April. The weather was great and there was still some snow at the top of the mountains, so they decided to go skiing the next day. The owner's son, Quentin, showed them around. It was wonderful. The next day Sally and Luke went riding. In the evening they all ate together and talked about life in New York and Montana. Sophie and Henry were beginning to think that moving to Montana would be the best thing that could ever happen to them. Even Sally was beginning to seem happier. After tea she disappeared with Quentin, and her mum hoped that she might already be forgetting about Mick. When Sally and Quentin came back, Sophie could see that Sally had been crying, but she looked happier.

F. A few months later ...
"I can't believe you're really going," said Lisa, "Don't you want to stay? I'm sure you could stay with us if I asked my parents."
"Oh, Lisa! I don't know what I want. I don't know if moving to Montana is a mistake or not. But I'm glad that you're my friend again."
"So am I. How could you think that I was in love with Mick? And him with me?"
"I don't know. When I saw you together at that party, what else could I think? You were lying with him on a sofa!"
"Yes, I know," said Lisa, laughing, "Somebody had pulled the carpet and we'd slipped. It was so funny. I didn't know you'd seen us. You didn't talk to me at all. You didn't even ask me."
"But you still stayed my friend. That's great. But Mick is still angry with me."
"Well, you shouldn't have told him about that guy in Montana. Are you looking forward to seeing him again?"
"Quentin? Yes, I think I am. But I'm worried about missing you."

2 In dem Text kommen etliche Charaktere vor. Ergänze die Namen neben den richtigen Aussagen: Sally, Mick, Luke, Sophie, Henry, Lisa oder Quentin?

1. He lives in Montana. ______________
2. He was Sally's boyfriend. ______________
3. He has lost his job. ______________
4. He wants his own horse. ______________
5. She can work from home. ______________
6. She's Sally's best friend. ______________
7. He's Sally's dad. ______________
8. She often talks to her friends on the phone. ______________

3 *True or false?* Kreuze richtig an. Dann korrigiere die falschen Sätze.

	true	false
1. Sally had not been very relaxed for a few weeks.	☐	☐
2. Sally's dad walked in when they were having dinner.	☐	☐
3. Sally's dad asked if he could move to Montana.	☐	☐
4. At first Sally and Luke didn't want to move to Montana.	☐	☐
5. Sally told her mum that she had split up with Mick.	☐	☐
6. Sally had thought that Lisa and Mick were in love with each other.	☐	☐
7. Sally liked Quentin.	☐	☐

Korrektur: ______________________________

____

____

Listening: Pros and cons of living in the country 11

4 Sallys Vater spricht abends nach dem Essen mit Quentins Eltern, Frank und Jenny. Höre dir den Dialog an und unterstreiche die richtigen Wörter.

1. Frank and Jenny moved to Montana from York/New York/Boston.
2. They moved six months/six years/sixteen years ago.
3. They had come out on holiday/for work/to look for a lodge one winter.
4. They have cows/pigs/rabbits and visitors at their lodge.
5. They miss/don't miss/hated their life in New York.
6. There were too little/too many/too few people in New York.
7. Frank misses the cinema/the subway/the snow.
8. Henry agrees/doesn't agree/understands when Frank explains why you don't notice the seasons in New York.

Writing: Sally's e-mail

5 Sieh dir Sallys Tagebuchnotizen an und vervollständige ihre E-Mail.

Hi Lisa, I'm slowly getting used to __________

__________. Everything ____________________

at first. ____________________ takes an hour

but Quentin ____________________.

I ____________________ river here. And

tomorrow ____________________.

I'm looking ____________________ there.

CU Sally

Monday:
Life getting better
but seems so slow.
Took an hour to get
to school.

Quentin drove me.

Swimming in river.

Tomorrow – rodeo!

Mediation and speaking: Small talk 12

6 Ihr macht Pause auf einem Berggipfel in Montana, als euch Leute begegnen. Was könntest du sagen? Überlege zuerst und schreibe deine Antworten auf, erst dann höre dir die CD an.

Mann: Hi.

Du: Erwidere die Begrüßung und sage, dass man hier oben einen schönen Blick hat: ______________________

____

Frau: Yes, it is. It's wonderful. And it was a hard hike up here.

Du: Stimme zu und sage, dass es sich gelohnt hat. Frage, ob sie ein Bild von euch machen könnten: ______________________

____

Mann: Yes, of course. How does it work? OK. There you are.

Du: Bedanke dich und frage, ob sie aus der Gegend kommen: __________

____

Mann: Yes, we're from Helena. We always come out to the mountains at the weekend.

Du: Äußere dein Interesse und frage ihn, ob sie einen Ort empfehlen würden, den du besichtigen könntest: ______________________

____

Frau: Yes, I'd visit the Big Belt Mountains if I were you. They are beautiful.

Du: Bedanke dich und beende die Unterhaltung: ______________________

____

Unit 4

Bilder

1 Beschrifte die Bilder korrekt.

a) ____________

b) ____________

c) ____________

d) ____________

Outdoor activities

2 Welche Aktivitäten sind gefragt? Ergänze die Buchstabenlücken.

1. Two sports which you need a rope for: a _ _ e _ _ _ _ g, _ l _ _ _ _ _ g
2. Two sports which you do on water: _ u _ _ _ n _, r _ w _ _ _
3. One sport which you need a compass for: _ r _ _ _ t _ _ _ _ _ _
4. One sport for which you need shoes with wheels on: _ _ _ _ _ _ g
5. One activity in which you carry a bag: b _ _ _ _ _ _ _ _ n _
6. Two sports for which you need good shoes: j _ _ _ _ _ _, _ _ k _ _ _

Filme

3 Trage die richtigen Wörter in das Kreuzworträtsel ein.

across:

1. The … is what happens through the play or film.
2. Information about the plot and the cast are typical … of a review.
3. The … is the person who tells the actors what to do.
4. You watch a big … in a cinema.
7. The … time is how long the film lasts.

down:

1. The … gives all the words that are spoken in the film.
4. The … was played by an excellent orchestra.
5. I always read a … before I go and see a film.
6. An … is a man who is in a film or play.
8. The … is the main story of a film.
9. A "U" … means that anybody can watch the film.
10. Famous stars don't usually have to go to a … to get a part in a film.

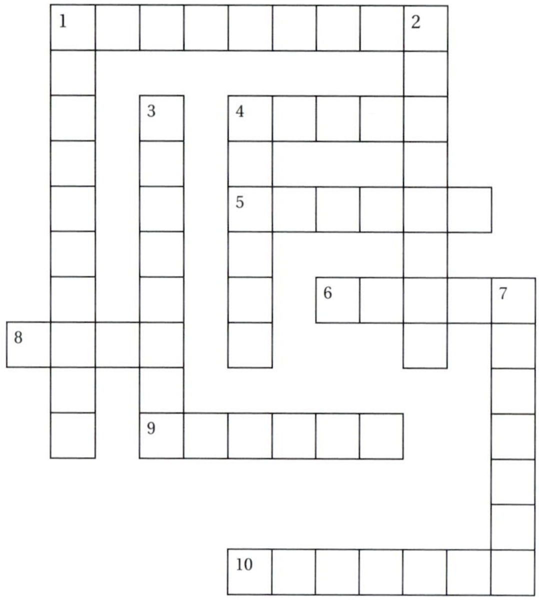

Abstrakte Substantive: Gefühle

4 Übersetze die folgenden Substantive.

Vorliebe	______________	Wunsch	______________
Freude	______________	Wert	______________
Gefühl	______________	Angst	______________

Adjektive

5 *Dimensions.* Welches Wort man verwendet, hängt davon ab, was man beschreibt. Notiere die richtigen Wörter.

1. The road is ______________.

2. The mountain is ______________.

3. The man is ______________.

6 *Opposites.* Löse die Anagramme auf und ordne sie ihrem Gegenteil zu.

vabre –tabledicpre – stany – valie

dead ______________ nice ______________

nervous ______________ surprising ______________

7 Adjektive mit den Endungen *-less* und *-ful*. Ergänze die Wörter wie angegeben und gib jeweils die Übersetzung dazu an.

noun	+ -less	+ -ful
help	______________	______________
joy	______________	______________
fear	______________	______________
end	______________	______________

Wichtige Wendungen: Befürchtungen äußern / jemandem helfen

8 Was könntest du auf die folgenden Zweifel oder Befürchtungen antworten? Bilde vollständige Sätze aus den angegebenen Wörtern.

about – rope – don't – worry – breaking – the

try – look – not – to – just – down

the – it – thing – to – to – is – do – think – not – best – about

first – difficult – most – time – is – always – the – the

1. When I think about jumping out of a plane, I don't think I'll be able to do it. – ______________________________.
2. I'm too scared to climb any higher. – We're almost there now. ______________________________.
3. I'm worried that I'll forget my words again when I go on stage. – Oh, you'll be fine. ______________________________.
4. I don't want to do it now. It would be awful if the rope broke. – ______________________________. It is too strong.

Verben

9 Mit welchen Substantiven kannst du diese Verben verwenden?

pull crash criticize dig quit solve

to ______________	a film	to ______________	a hole
to ______________	a problem	to ______________	a bag on wheels
to ______________	a plane	to ______________	a job

Der Infinitiv (Wiederholung)

Der **Infinitiv** ist die Grundform des Verbs. Man kann ihn mit und ohne *to* verwenden.

Der Infinitiv **ohne *to*** wird hauptsächlich mit Modalverben verwendet:
I should **do** more sport.
She can't **climb** that cliff.

Der Infinitiv **mit *to*** folgt auf verschiedene Verben, Adjektive und Nomen:
– nach Verben (z. B. *want, decide* und *would like*):
I **want to go** home now.
– nach Adjektiven (z. B. *dangerous, easy, better* und *worse*):
It's **dangerous to climb** without a rope.
– nach Nomen (z. B. *the chance, the way, the idea, the wish, time*):
He had the **idea to sail** the Atlantic.

Alle Verben außer den modalen Hilfsverben haben einen Infinitiv.

10 In den *Rockies*. Benötigen die Verben in Klammern *to* oder nicht? Trage ein.

Chris loves the outdoors so when he was offered the chance ______ (work) in a camp in the Rockies, it wasn't difficult ______ (decide). It's hard work. He must ______ (get up) early every day and he works till late. But in his free time he can ______ (do) what he likes. He's finished work when he suddenly has the idea ______ (walk) to the top of the mountain so that he can see the sunset. He forgets that he will have to ______ (come) down again in the dark. The sunset is amazing and Chris feels happy when it's time ______ (go) home but when he tries ______ (find) the way, he can't ______ (do) it. He has to ______ (stay) on the mountain all night. He's scared but when the sun comes up the next morning, he is glad that he has been such an idiot.

Der Infinitiv mit *to*

Den **Infinitiv mit *to*** verwendest du, wenn du möchtest, dass jemand etwas macht. Es gilt **Verb + Objekt + Infinitiv:**

He **asked her to send** him a picture. ("Send me a picture.")
They **expect people to behave** well in the park. ("Behave well in the park!")

Den Infinitiv mit *to* verwendet man auch nach **Fragewörtern:**
I have no idea **what to do** when I see a bear.
Do you know **which way to go?**
They wondered **whether** *(ob)* **to go home** again.

Der Infinitiv mit *to* steht auch nach *the first, the last, the only one* und Superlativen:

He was **the first (man) to get** to the top.
They were **the only ones to make it** home again.
That's the **biggest fish to be caught** this year.

Solche Sätze übersetzt du am besten mit einem Relativsatz:

Er war **der erste Mensch, der** auf den Gipfel gelangte. Sie waren **die einzigen, die** es wieder nach Hause schafften.

11 *Orienteering.* Unterstreiche den Infinitiv mit *to* und begründe, warum er verwendet wird.

1. She wanted to try a new sport.
2. She went orienteering but didn't know how to find her way.
3. She wondered whether to go left or right.
4. She asked a girl to show her.
5. The girl showed her how to read a map.
6. It was more difficult to do than she had thought.
7. She was the last one to finish.

12 *My perfect climbing holiday*. Formuliere die folgenden Sätze mit dem Infinitiv mit *to* neu.

1. My friends should come with me.

→ I want my friends to come with me.

2. I hope my holiday will be exciting.

→ I'd like ______________________.

3. I can't climb.

→ I don't know ______________________.

4. The teachers should teach us well.

→ I expect ______________________.

5. I hope I won't be the only person who is scared.

→ I hope I won't be ______________________.

13 *Alone on holiday*. Übersetze die folgenden Sätze ins Englische.

Ella war meine erste Freundin, die alleine in die Ferien gefahren ist.

Ella was ______________________ alone.

Sie wusste nicht, was sie mitnehmen sollte.

______________________ with her.

Wir rieten ihr, ihr Handy und ein wenig Geld mitzunehmen.

____

Ihre Eltern erwarteten, dass sie vorsichtig sein würde.

____

Gerund oder Infinitiv nach bestimmten Verben 1

Das ***gerund*** kann als Subjekt oder Objekt eines Satzes stehen, nach bestimmten Verben/Adjektiven + Präposition sowie nach bestimmten Verben, z. B. *to start, to begin, to like, to prefer, to love, to hate, can't stand, to enjoy, to mind, to keep, to risk, to imagine:*

It **started snowing** when we left.

Neben dem *gerund* kannst du bei folgenden Verben auch den **Infinitiv mit *to*** verwenden: *to decide, to want, would like, to start, to begin, to like, to prefer, to love, to hate:*

I **decided to do** some homework.

Nach bestimmten Verben haben das *gerund* und der Infinitiv die **gleiche Bedeutung,** z. B. nach *to start, to begin, to like, to prefer, to love, to hate:*

I **like to eat** chips = I **like eating** chips.

14 *The movies.* Lies den Text und unterstreiche die richtige Form des Verbs: *gerund,* Infinitiv oder beides?

I love going/to go to the movies. I'd love being/to be in the movies myself but I'm not very good at acting/to act. Before I decide what watching/to watch, I read all the reviews. That's the best way finding/to find the best films, I think.

I like buying/to buy my ticket very early and then I go into the cinema before everybody else starts coming/to come in. When I'm the first person going/to go in, I can choose the best seat. I prefer sitting/to sit quite near the front but not too near. I have my favourite seat so I don't have to wonder where sitting/to sit for too long. And do you know what I really hate? I hate people eating/to eat crisps while I'm watching the film.

Gerund oder Infinitiv nach bestimmten Verben 2

Je nachdem, ob ein *gerund* oder ein Infinitiv folgt, haben diese Verben **unterschiedliche Bedeutung:**

to stop und ***to go on:***
+ Infinitiv → Ende einer Handlung/Anfang einer neuen Handlung:
You need **to stop to eat** something (aufhören, um etwas zu essen).
After dinner I **went on to play** tennis (spielte nach dem Essen …).
+ *gerund* → Aufhören/Weitermachen mit der ursprünglichen Aktion:
Please **stop talking**. — Bitte hör auf zu reden.
I can **go on walking** for miles. — Ich kann noch … weitergehen (= werde nicht müde …).

to forget und ***to remember*:**
+ Infinitiv → Etwas muss noch passieren:
Please don't **forget**/Please **remember to write** me (= dass du noch schreiben musst).
+ *gerund* → Etwas ist bereits passiert:
He won't **forget**/will **remember meeting** Ann (= dass er sie getroffen hat).

to mean und ***to try:***
I mean **to work harder**. — Ich beabsichtige, härter zu arbeiten.
That **means watching** less TV. — Das bedeutet, weniger TV …
I **tried to call** her. — Ich versuchte, sie anzurufen.
Try calling her on her cell phone. — Probier mal, sie auf ihrem Handy zu erreichen.

15 *A first girlfriend.* Unterstreiche die richtige Verbform, damit die Übersetzung stimmt.

1. I mustn't forget buying/to buy her a birthday present.

   Ich darf nicht vergessen, ihr ein Geburtstagsgeschenk zu kaufen.

2. I'll never forget meeting/to meet her the very first time.

   Ich werde nie das erste Mal vergessen, als ich sie getroffen habe.

3. I was playing football and I saw her when I stopped having/to have a drink.

   Ich spielte Fußball und sah sie, als ich aufhörte, um etwas zu trinken.

16 *In a canoe.* Ordne die richtigen Sätze einander zu.

1. Look after yourself. Be careful.

2. The water's not very deep, is it?

3. Oh no. I haven't told my mum where she should pick us up.

4. We can't use the phone here because there's no signal.

5. We can't put the canoe back in the water there. It's still not deep enough.

a) I forgot to call her this morning.

b) I tried to use my cell phone.

c) Remember to wear a helmet.

d) We'll have to go on carrying it.

e) No, it'll mean carrying the canoe in some places.

→ 1. ______; 2. ______; 3. ______; 4. ______; 5. ______

Zuhören: *In the mountains* 13

17 Höre dir die verschiedenen Abschnitte des Dialogs an und unterstreiche dann die zutreffenden Verben, um den Gesprächsinhalt richtig wiederzugeben.

1. He'll try going/to go to the left.

2. They're going to stop eating/to eat something.

3. They went on getting/to get to the top.

4. They meant bringing/to bring the camera.

5. They'll remember getting/to get to the top for a long time.

Indirekte Rede (Wiederholung)

Steht das **einleitende Verb in der Vergangenheit** (z. B. *said, told*), findet im Folgesatz der indirekten Rede eine Verschiebung der Zeiten statt. Sonst gibt es keine Zeitverschiebung.

"I **like** climbing." → She **said she liked** climbing.

simple present → simple past

present progressive → past progressive

simple past/present perfect/past perfect → past perfect

will → would; can → could

Auch die Pronomen müssen entsprechend geändert werden:

"**I** can't hear **you.**" → She said **she** couldn't hear **us.**

Zeit- und **Ortsangaben** werden abhängig vom Standpunkt geändert:

"I'll see you **here tomorrow.**"→ He said he'd see us **there the day after.**

Bei **Fragen** werden die Hilfsverben *do, does* und *did* nicht verwendet. Die Satzstellung ist dieselbe wie in Aussagesätzen:

"**Where did you go** yesterday?" → He asked me **where I went ...**

Wenn die **Frage kein Fragewort** beinhaltet, wird im Folgesatz *if* oder *whether* verwendet:

"**Do you like** it here?" → She asked me **if I liked** it there.

Aufforderungssätze werden als Infinitivkonstruktion mit ***to*** oder ***not to*** wiedergegeben:

"**Don't drive** too fast." → They warned us **not to drive** too fast.

18 John und Lisa unterhalten sich. Gib die Sätze in indirekter Rede wieder.

1. "Do you like the States?"

   He asked ______________________________.

2. "I've never been there."

   She answered ______________________________.

3. "Would you like to go with me?" *(→ invite!)*

   He ______________________________.

19 *Watching TV.* Berichte, was gesprochen wurde.

1. She asked ______________________________.

2. He answered ______________________________.

3. He asked ______________________________.

4. She answered ______________________________.

5. He told her ______________________________.

Zuhören: *A climbing holiday* 14

20 Kylie will mit Alex in die Ferien fahren. Höre dir zunächst das Gespräch zwischen ihr und ihrer Mutter an. Beim zweiten Hören vervollständige die Lücken.

Kylie asked her mum ______ she ______ go on a climbing holiday with Alex.

Her mum answered she __________ know and that climbing __________ very dangerous.

Kylie said that her mum ______________ climbing ________________.

Her mum agreed but said that it ______________ very dangerous.

Her mum then asked _______ she ___________ to pay for it.

Kylie said that she _______________ enough money.

Her Mum said OK but that she _______________ be very careful.

Lesen: *A movie review*

Filmkritik
Eine Filmkritik beinhaltet Informationen über den Film, Fakten über den Regisseur, die Schauspieler, die Handlung, die Laufzeit und die Altersfreigabe. Der Kritiker äußert außerdem seine Meinung.
Lerne zu unterscheiden zwischen den bloßen Tatsachen und der Meinung des Kritikers. Jeder sieht einen Film anders – letztlich musst du dir selbst ein Bild von dem Film machen.

21 Lies die Filmkritik, dann vervollständige die Tabelle mit den Fakten.

A Christmas Carol – 96 minutes, USA (2009)
This is the latest film of Charles Dickens' book with the same title. It is a 3-D remake of the old classic Christmas film.
The story is about Ebenezer Scrooge (Jim Carrey) who is mean to everybody and hates Christmas. It takes place in London in the 19th century, a time when many people were poor and life was hard. Ebenezer's nephew (*Neffe*), played by Colin Firth, needs help on the night before Christmas but Ebenezer is not interested in helping anybody. That night he is visited by four ghosts who show him that he needs to change.
Jim Carrey is the star of the film and shows his acting abilities (*Fähigkeiten*), but unfortunately the other actors, especially Colin Firth, Bill Murray and Gary Oldman, are not given the chance to shine by director Robert Zemeckis. The 3-D special effects work well in this film and it is definitely scary when the ghosts come out of the screen. The film-rating is PG, but parents be warned: young children might find the film quite frightening.
The film has some funny moments but it is really almost as serious as the book. Unfortunately the ending, which is warm-hearted in the book, is quite cold in this film. All in all, this film is to be recommended only for technology fans.

Title:			
Running time:		Rating:	
Director:			
Cast:			
Who is it recommended for?			

22 *Fact or opinion?* Lies die folgenden Sätze: Handelt es sich um Tatsachen oder um die Meinung des Kritikers? Kreuze an.

	fact	opinion
1. Ebenezer Scrooge is not friendly.	☐	☐
2. Four ghosts visit Scrooge.	☐	☐
3. Jim Carrey is the star of the film.	☐	☐
4. Jim Carrey acts well.	☐	☐
5. Zemeckis doesn't allow Colin Firth to show his abilities.	☐	☐
6. The film is very scary.	☐	☐
7. The film rating is PG.	☐	☐
8. Charles Dickens' book is serious.	☐	☐

23 Was trifft zu? Unterstreiche.

1. The story takes place in the 1800s/1900s in London/Paris.
2. Most of the story takes place the night before/after Christmas.
3. Charles Dickens is an actor/a director/a writer.
4. The four ghosts show Scrooge he needs to become richer/kinder/poorer.
5. Small children aren't allowed to watch the film with/without parents.
6. The writer of the review liked none/some/all of the film.

Lesen: *Types of texts*

24 Lies die drei Texte, dann ordne zu: Welches Bild passt zu welchem Text?

1. ______; 2. ______; 3. ______

A. Joseph Plant, the well-known movie star, has gone missing. He was last seen on Monday morning in the Rockies. The police have been looking for him since his wife reported him missing. Plant, who is an excellent climber, often flies out to the Rockies and spends a weekend climbing alone, his wife said this morning. He had his cell phone with him and his wife is worried that he has been attacked or been badly hurt. No signs have been found so far.

B. *Run, Lola, Run* is a German film which was an international success. It is about a girl who has 20 minutes to find 100,000 DM (about 50,000 Euros). If she doesn't manage to find the money, her boyfriend may be killed by his gangster boss. The film takes place in Berlin in the 1990s. It is exciting and funny and is full of surprises. Franka Potente and Moritz Bleibtreu, who play the two main characters, are excellent, and the film has a modern feel to it even after so many years. Definitely to be recommended.

C. Alice Bennet is one of the best climbers ever. She grew up in New Zealand, the youngest of three children. Her parents, both teachers, were always interested in outdoor activities, although they preferred water sports to climbing. Bennet first got interested in climbing on a school trip when she was 18 and since then she has never stopped. She dreams of climbing every mountain in the world over 8000 metres.

25 Um welche Art von Texten handelt es sich?

A. ________________ B. ________________

C. ________________

26 Lies die Texte noch einmal und beantworte die folgenden Fragen dazu.

1. What is Joseph Plant's job? ________________
2. What was Plant doing in the Rockies? ________________
3. Why did Plant's wife think he may have been attacked or be badly hurt? ________________
4. Who are the main actors in *Run, Lola, Run*? ________________
5. What does the writer of the review think about the film? ________________
6. How many brothers and sisters does Alice Bennet have? ________________
7. What do Alice's parents do? ________________
8. When did Alice learn to climb? ________________

Zuhören: *Expressing fears and being positive* 15

27 Höre dir die Dialoge an, dann ordne sie der richtigen Situation zu.

a) Abseiling ________ c) At a casting ________

b) In a canoe ________ d) On a date ________

28 *Expressing fears.* Höre dir CD-Track 15 nochmals an. In welchem Dialog hörst du die folgenden Wendungen?

1. When I think about it, my knees feel weak. ________
2. I'm too scared to go on. ________
3. Oh, I wish I hadn't agreed to do this. ________
4. I'm too scared to go over that cliff. ________
5. But now I'm worried that my friends will laugh at me. ________

29 *Being positive.* Wie wird versucht, den Gesprächspartner zu beruhigen? Vervollständige die Wendungen.

Dialogue 1:

But don't ________. It'll be ________. ________ be safe.

Dialogue 2:

The best thing ________ is just to ________ them if they laugh at you.

Dialogue 3:

I'm ________ the first ________ is always the ________.

Dialogue 4:

Just ________ look down. You can ________ it.

30 Lies die Fragen und wähle die richtige(n) Antwort(en) aus.

1. Why can't the man in the canoe go back?
a) The water is too strong.
b) The water is too deep.
c) The rocks are too big. → ________

2. The woman says when he has done it once, he'll want to do it again because …
a) being scared is great.
b) it's great fun.
c) it's not scary. → ________

3. The boy doesn't want to go to the party because …
a) he thinks his friends will laugh at him.
b) he thinks Kate will laugh at him.
c) he doesn't want Kate to think he is an idiot. → ________

4. The boy thinks the casting …
a) is a waste of time.
b) is a great chance for the girl.
c) is good practice. → ________

5. The girl wants the director …
a) to think she's good.
b) not to see her at all.
c) not to think she's bad. → ________

6. How are they going to go down the cliff?
a) With special shoes.
b) On a rope.
c) slowly. → ________

7. What does the man say the woman will have when she has done it once?
a) Less fear.
b) More happiness.
c) More confidence. → ________

Revision C (Standards)

Standardprüfung Green Line 3
Reading: Tour of the USA

1 Matt macht eine Tour durch die USA. An seine Freunde zu Hause schreibt er E-Mails. Lies sie und bringe sie in die richtige Reihenfolge.

Reihenfolge: 1 ___; 2. ___; 3. ___; 4. ___

(A) Hi Ann,
We made it all the way across the States and tomorrow we're flying back home again. San Francisco and Los Angeles are great. And guess what! I saw Cheryl Lacey – you remember, in that film we saw – last week in a café. We had just finished lunch and in she walked. I said hello, but it was very embarrassing because she just ignored me. Mum, Dad and Helen all laughed at me.
I can't believe I've already been here for six weeks, but I'm really glad I came. If I hadn't come, I would have still thought that America is a country full of police officers, cowboys and Indians and film stars.
See you soon.

(B) Hi Rob,
We got to New York on Monday. The flight from London was terrible. We had to land in Greenland on the way, so we were very late and we arrived in New York at 3 a.m. And the funny thing was that there were still lots of cars and lots of people on the streets. It's true – "New York never sleeps". It's really exciting actually and it's so funny to see all the places which you see in films. I always expect to see a famous actor getting out of a taxi. And every time I hear a police car, I think there'll be a police car chase or somebody will start shooting. Actually though, people say New York is really safe now.

(C) Hi Ann,
We're staying with my cousins in Chicago now. Jeanie says hello and she's invited you to come and visit, too. Chicago's cool. It's on Lake Michigan and there are some great beaches around the lake which we've been to a few times. We've had to go really because it's so hot at the moment. We haven't got the energy to do anything else. But tomorrow we're going to go to a baseball match. Yuk! I'm not really interested but my uncle says it'll be fun. Well, they watched a cricket match in England, so I have to go.

(D) Hi Rob,
We've been here for four weeks now and we've already driven half way across the USA to Missouri. We're hoping to see the Grand Canyon on Saturday. It's so different here. The people have really strong accents and they like to laugh at ours. Chicago and New York seem really European in comparison. We're staying on a farm now and yesterday I had a ride on a really big tractor. The farm is really big so they need it. They're a long way from shops here, so they grow almost everything they need themselves.

2 Lies die E-Mails ein zweites Mal, dann beantworte die folgenden Fragen.

1. Where did Matt fly from and to?
2. What time did he land?
3. What did he see in New York?
4. What was the weather like in Chicago?
5. Which sport did they watch in Chicago?
6. What did the people in Missouri laugh at?
7. Where did the people on the farm get their food from?
8. What did they visit after Missouri?
9. What is Cheryl Lacey's job?
10. How long did they stay in the USA?

3 Lies Anns Beschreibung von Matts Ferien. Finde die inhaltlichen Fehler, streiche sie durch und korrigiere sie auf der rechten Seite.

My friend Matt flew across America this year with his parents and he really hated it. He said that it's true that New York never sleeps because there are never lots of people around. He said it was exciting and dangerous there. After New York he visited friends in Chicago and he loved swimming in the sea there. In Los Angeles he saw Cheryl Lacey in a film. He said that he was glad he had visited because now he knew that the USA was full of police officers, film stars and cowboys and Indians.

Writing and mediation: An e-mail

4 Matts Cousine, Jeanie, hat ihre deutsche Brieffreundin Mara eingeladen. Schau dir Jeanies E-Mail an Mara an, dann verfasse aus Maras Notizen eine E-Mail an Jeanie.

Hi Mara,
How are you? Did you enjoy yourself in England?
The holidays have been great up to now. My cousin Matt was here last week. We were lucky because the weather was really hot and we spent a lot of time on the beach. My cousin loved it here and he even loved the baseball match which he hadn't wanted to watch.
It's quiet here now and I'm really happy that you are coming here next week.
My dad has some questions for you.
When does your plane land? Is there anything you don't eat? How long are your parents going to stay with you?
Are you excited, too? Please write soon.
CU (soon), ☺
Jeanie.

Danke. Super in England.
Tante wohnt in Manchester.
Wales besucht: überall verschiedene Akzente!! Kann dich hoffentlich verstehen.
Cricketmatch angeschaut – Regeln wie Baseball?
Ganz aufgeregt! Lande 10. August, 17.30 Uhr. Abholen?
Esse alles. Eltern bleiben bis 14. – OK?

Hi Jeanie,

Listening: Telephone messages 16

5 *Jeanie's answering machine.* Auf Jeanies Anrufbeantworter gehen mehrere Nachrichten ein. Höre sie dir an, dann beantworte die Fragen.

1. Why does Matt phone? ______________________
2. What should Jeanie do? ______________________
3. Who was the second message from? ______________________
4. Where did he have a problem? ______________________
5. What does he have to do? ______________________
6. What did Sara want? ______________________
   ____
7. What number should Jeanie phone? ______________________

Speaking: Apologising and helping 17

6 *At the airport.* Überlege zunächst, was du in den folgenden Situationen sagen könntest. Trage deine Sätze ein. Dann höre dir die CD an.

1. You stand on somebody's foot.

   ____

2. You see an old woman with very heavy bags.

   ____

3. You want to go to the information desk but don't know where it is. Ask a man.

   ____

4. The man shows you the way to the information desk.

   ____

Standardprüfung Green Line 4
Reading: Skiing in the Rockies

7 Lies den Text über Alices Skiferien und entscheide dich für eine Überschrift.

A. Love story on skis ☐ B. How my camera saved my life ☐

C. How my boyfriend saved my life ☐ D. Broken skis and a broken leg ☐

I'm not great at skiing but I really enjoy it – now. When I moved to Montana from New York a few years ago, I had never been skiing before and wasn't too crazy on the idea. My parents and my brother did some ski courses but I told them skiing definitely wasn't for me. How can you know if you never try it? they asked. But I knew that snow was cold and wet and I couldn't understand why anybody should want to spend a whole day outside in it. That was before I met Aaron.
Aaron was one cool dude and he loved skiing. Everybody said he was bad at it – he looked as though he was fighting with his skis, people said – but he loved it. In the holidays some guys from my class were going skiing together and Aaron asked me if I wanted to go, too. I couldn't say no. I said yes but then I was worried about making an idiot of myself so I decided to take some lessons on my own first.
I don't know when I started enjoying skiing, but I think it might have been when I saw how attractive the ski instructor was. Or was it when I noticed that actually the snow isn't really cold and wet in the mountains? Or was it when I saw the beautiful views, or when I skied down a slope by myself for the first time and it felt amazing? Anyway I loved it and was looking forward to going on my first skiing holiday more than ever.
We all stayed in a big lodge in the mountains. The views were fantastic and the snow was great. In the mornings we skied down to the ski lifts and I did a ski course while my friends were skiing on the slopes. In the afternoons I joined my friends, but they were a lot better than me so I got tired more quickly than they did and I often had a break outside a mountain café.
The last day came and we all decided to take our bags down in the lift, leave them in the cars and then ski all day until it went dark. It was a wonderful day and we didn't want it to end but about 4 pm. Gemma decided she wanted to go home and she set off with three friends in the car. I was quite tired by then, but Aaron wanted to carry on skiing and the day was so wonderful that I decided to do another run, too. I hadn't noticed the clouds coming up from the west. We went up in the lift and then set off down again. At first it was fun but then we skied into a cloud and I couldn't see anything. I fell over. The others, who were still a lot better at skiing than me, were in front of me and didn't see me. Soon I was on my own. Or I felt like I was on my own. If somebody had been ten metres away, I wouldn't have seen them because of the fog. I didn't even know which way to go.

There were flags at the edges of the slopes but I couldn't see them. I called out but nobody answered. Everything seemed very quiet. It seemed like everybody had gone home and left me. I had to try to follow the ski tracks. That was easier said than done. It was difficult to ski slowly and I kept falling over. Suddenly I saw somebody. I called out but they had disappeared before I even opened my mouth. How could they ski so fast in the fog? At least I was going the right way, I thought. I carried on but suddenly the snow disappeared from under me. I was flying with my skis on and I had no idea where I would land.

I landed in soft, deep snow but my right leg had hit something, maybe a tree. It hurt and the ski had come off. I looked around for the ski but I couldn't find it. It was probably under the snow somewhere. Then I noticed that the fog had cleared. I had come out of the cloud and now I could see the mountainside and down into the valley. But I couldn't see any people or any marked ski slopes. Oh no, how was I going to get down the mountain? I got my mobile phone out but it wasn't working. I stood up and then fell down again because of the pain in my right leg. My leg looked strange and I was sure that I must have broken it. I put some snow on my leg to stop the pain and thought. In films when people broke their leg, they tied it to a stick and then they could walk on it. Would that work in real life? I had nothing to lose so I tried it. It worked. I could stand on it a little.

Now I just had to get down the mountain. If somebody had told me that by the end of the day I would be able to ski on one ski through deep snow, I wouldn't have believed them. But I could. Very slowly I moved down the mountain. I often fell over but I just got up again and carried on. The worse thing now was that it was getting dark and I still had no idea how to get help or where I was.

When I got to the bottom of the mountain, I was so happy that I started laughing. But now what? I looked around and tried to work out which way to go. I chose the easiest way and after some time I came to a road. I hoped I would see somebody soon, but there were no cars, no houses, nothing. I kept going. I had no idea what time it was, how long I had been missing, what my friends were doing, or how long I would be able to survive. The nights were very cold and I was beginning to feel cold already. Surely I wouldn't be able to survive a night out here! I kept going. Sometimes my eyes closed and I fell over. I was so tired I wanted to stay there on the soft snow and close my eyes but I forced myself to get up and go on.

Then I heard a helicopter. Was it looking for me? Oh no. It wouldn't see me. What could I do? And suddenly I had an idea. I got out my camera and took photos into the sky. It flashed *(blitzen)*. I did it again and again. The helicopter came nearer. It had seen me. I cheered. Then it flew away. I couldn't believe it. I fell down onto the ground and cried and cried. I couldn't move any more. I would die. My eyes closed.

Ten minutes later, they told me afterwards, the rescue team arrived on their motor sleds. The helicopter hadn't been able to land but they had told the rescue team where I was. I was taken to hospital and I had to spend the night there. I had been out on the mountain for nine hours, but I had survived and now I had a story to tell which would surprise people for the rest of my life.

8 Lies die Sätze und entscheide, ob sie *true*, *false* oder *not in the text* sind. Dann korrigiere die falschen Sätze.

	true	false	not in the text
1. Alice comes from New York.	☐	☐	☐
2. She didn't want to go skiing because she didn't like the snow.	☐	☐	☐
3. Aaron wasn't very good at skiing.	☐	☐	☐
4. Alice had ski lessons.	☐	☐	☐
5. She had breaks more often because she was lazy.	☐	☐	☐
6. Until 4 pm on the last day the weather was good.	☐	☐	☐
7. Alice didn't know which way to go because she was on her own.	☐	☐	☐
8. She skied off the slope because it was faster that way.	☐	☐	☐
9. She skied down the mountain on one ski.	☐	☐	☐
10. The helicopter found her because of the light from her camera.	☐	☐	☐

Korrektur:

Writing: A newspaper report

9 Vervollständige den Zeitungsbericht über Alices Abenteuer. Verwende dazu Informationen aus dem Text und die folgenden Zitate.

"We noticed that she was missing and went back to look for her."
"We couldn't find her anywhere."
"We skied to the bottom of the mountain and waited for her."
"When she didn't arrive, we called the rescue number."
"She's doing fine in hospital and we hope she will be able to come home today."

Mountain Rescue

Last night just after 1 o'clock ______________________________

______________________ in which she broke her leg and lost her way.

She is now ______________________________

__________.

The accident happened just after 4 pm yesterday afternoon when ________

____

____

Her friends noticed that she was missing ______________________

____

____

____

______________________________. Alice tied her

____

____

______________________ when she used her camera to flash into the sky.

Mediation and speaking: Small talk

10 Du bist mit deinen Eltern in einem Café in den Rockies. Ihr wollt euch zu einer Frau an den Tisch setzen. Hilf beim Übersetzen.

Vater: Frag sie bitte, ob wir uns dazusetzen können.

Du: ____________________

Frau: Yes, of course. May I ask you where you are from?

Du: (Ihr seid aus Süddeutschland:) ____________________

____

Frau: Oh, that's interesting. You're a long way from home.

Du: (Ja, aber ihr habt gehört, dass man in den Rockies gut Skifahren kann:) ____________________

Frau: Yes, that's right. And do you like it here?

Mutter: Ja. Die Pisten sind fantastisch und die Leute freundlich.

Du: ____________________

Listening: Small talk in the mountains 18

11 Hör dir Alices Gespräch mit Jody in einem Café an und beantworte die Fragen.

1. How long had Jody been skiing? ____________________
2. What did Jody once train for? ____________________
3. Why didn't she ski in the event? ____________________
4. Who did she meet in hospital? ____________________

Unit 5

California

1 Finde die elf Wörter in der Buchstabenschlange und trage sie richtig ein.

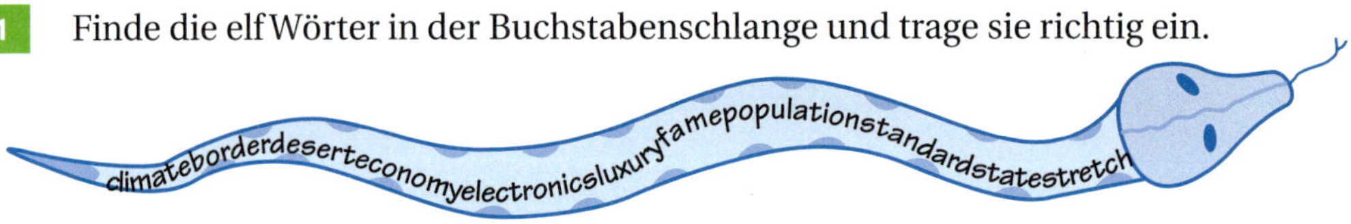

California is in the southwest of the USA and has a ____________ with Mexico to the south. It has the highest ____________ of all the American states because it has some very big cities and it is the third largest state. Its ____________ is very mixed with the areas near the coast wetter and cooler than those to the east. California is a very beautiful state with a fantastic ____________ of coast in the west, mountains in the middle and a ____________ in the east. The many national parks in California have kept much of the land in its natural ____________. California's ____________ is usually one of the strongest in the world but the ____________ of living in California is also very mixed. Many people have become very rich from the ____________ business or from their ____________ in the world of films and they live in ____________ but many others, especially illegal immigrants, don't have enough to eat.

Tipp Lies nicht nur bis zur Lücke im Text, sondern auch darüber hinaus, dann kommst du leichter darauf, welches Wort du einsetzen musst.

Adjektive und Adverbien

2 *Opposites.* Welche Wörter mit einer (fast) gegenteiligen Bedeutung kannst du für diese Vokabeln finden? Nenne je zwei.

ugly ______________________

well ______________________

clever ______________________

strange ______________________

3 Suche acht Adjektive aus dem Wortgitter heraus und ergänze sie in den passenden Sätzen.

E	X	C	L	U	S	I	V	E	Z	P
P	A	R	Z	R	K	L	P	J	H	R
A	U	I	C	G	O	L	D	E	N	I
I	V	M	H	I	A	E	H	D	F	V
N	K	I	P	Z	R	G	E	F	C	A
F	O	N	A	D	D	A	D	U	L	T
U	C	A	S	U	A	L	D	R	I	E
L	M	L	N	X	S	L	Z	C	R	K

It's __________ to steal.

It's __________ to waste water in California but not always illegal.

Are you going to wear __________ clothes to the party?

I don't think it's fair to have __________ beaches – they should be for everybody.

I love __________ sandy beaches.

When sand is very hot, it is __________ to walk on it.

People don't always become more __________ when they get older.

That's a very __________ restaurant – we can't eat there.

Verben

4 Übersetze die folgenden Verben.

belassen	______________	fallen lassen	______________
unterstützen	______________	verschwenden	______________
anziehen	______________	sausen	______________
bewachen	______________	annehmen	______________
genehmigen	______________	fluchen	______________
anstarren	______________	danken	______________
gießen	______________		

5 *Politics on the beach.* Welche Präpositionen folgen auf die Verben? Trage ein.

I have never been involved ______ politics at all but I do love surfing so when a friend called __________ a meeting on a beach, I was the first to show ______. The beach was public until a rich film star bought the land. The first we knew was when they closed ______ the beach last week. Somebody had already built a fence and put ______ a sign which said it was illegal to step ______ the beach. We had a party on the beach that night and we stayed ______ until the morning. It turned ______ to be the best party I've ever been to. We're going to work now until the beach is made public again. I never knew that politics was such fun!

Phrasal verbs

6 In jedem Satz fehlt ein Verb. Es ist jeweils das gleiche, es folgt ihm aber jedesmal eine andere Präposition. Trage das gesuchte Verb in die Lücken ein (Achtung Zeitform!), dann nenne die *phrasal verbs* nochmals in ihrer Grundform und übersetze sie.

1. I ________ **up** yesterday – late –, ran to the bus stop, ________ **on** the bus.

   I only realized it was Saturday when I ________ **to** school.

   ____

   ____

2. I went home, ______ **off** my best clothes and _____ **out** the dog for a walk.

   ____

   ____

3. That evening I watched a film I hoped was a comedy but it ________ **out** to be a thriller and very scary. When the hero ________ **into** a monster, I ________ **off** the TV and called a friend.

   ____

   ____

4. I called Ann and asked her to ________ **over.** She answered that she'd like to but her cousin was staying with her. I said that the cousin should ________ **along,** too. Five minutes later the door bell rang and I told them to ________ **in.**

   ____

   ____

Wichtige Wendungen: *Being polite / showing feelings*

7 Lies die informellen Sätze und vervollständige die höflichere Version der gleichen Aussage.

1. Hey, what's up?

→ Nice ____.

2. Sorry, what did you say?

→ I'm __________, could you ______________________________?

3. Hi, is Ella there?

__________, could I ________________________________?

4. Hey, could you give me a hand?

→ ____________ me, could ____________________________?

8 Bilde aus den angegebenen Wörtern ganze Sätze und ordne sie der passenden Situation zu.

doing – you – what – are – there – ?

know – stare – don't – to – you – it's – rude – ?

back – there – starts – hey, – the – line

1. You're waiting to be served and somebody pushes in in front of you.

____

2. Somebody is looking at you and you don't like it.

____

3. You see somebody stealing something.

____

Notwendige Relativsätze (Wiederholung)

Ein **notwendiger Relativsatz bestimmt** sein Bezugswort **näher:**

I love the actor **who was in Harry Potter.**

– Ohne den Relativsatz wäre der Satz nicht vollständig. *I love the actor* allein wäre bedeutungslos, da man nicht weiß, von welchem Schauspieler die Rede ist.

– Zwischen Relativsatz und Hauptsatz gibt es weder Kommas noch Sprechpausen.

Im Relativsatz steht normalerweise ein Pronomen. ***Who*** oder ***that*** wird für Personen verwendet, ***which*** oder ***that*** für Dinge oder Tiere. ***Whose*** verwendet man, um einen Besitz auszudrücken:

I want to buy a cell phone **which** isn't too expensive.
That's the man **whose** dog bit me yesterday.

Man braucht kein Relativpronomen, wenn es das Objekt des Relativsatzes ist:

That's the guy (who) Jane is going out with.

9 *At a Hollywood party*. Unterstreiche das richtige Relativpronomen. Tipp: Manchmal gibt es mehr als eine richtige Antwort.

Orlando: Hey, is that the actress which/–/who was in "Titanic"?

Cherry: You're right. Was "Titanic" that film which/–/who won lots of Oscars?

Orlando: Yes, and it was one of the first films which/–/who I saw at the movies.

Cherry: It was a true story about a ship which/–/who sank, wasn't it?

Orlando: Yes, and there was a captain which/–/who went down with his ship.

Cherry: And wasn't there a band which/–/who played while the ship went down?

Orlando: That's something which/–/who I couldn't do.

Cherry: But I wouldn't like to be a person which/–/who dies a hero.

Orlando: No. I just want to be the person which/–/who is the hero in the film.

Nicht-notwendige Relativsätze

Ein **nicht-notwendiger Relativsatz** gibt lediglich **zusätzliche Informationen** über sein Bezugswort:

Leo, **who is my favourite actor,** is starring in two new films.
California, **which is one of the biggest states,** has problems with water.

In nicht-notwendigen Relativsätzen
- wäre der Hauptsatz auch ohne den Relativsatz vollständig,
- gibt es immer Kommas zwischen Hauptsatz und Relativsatz,
- wird beim Sprechen eine Pause gemacht,
- kann man das Relativpronomen *that* nicht verwenden,
- muss man immer ein Relativpronomen verwenden.

Whose kann für Personen und Dinge verwendet werden:

California, **whose** biggest town is Los Angeles, has a big population.
Nancy Sinatra, **whose** father was Frank, is a singer and actress.

10 Bilde aus den zwei Sätzen einen Hauptsatz mit Relativsatz.

1. Jorge is an immigrant. He is from Mexico.

2. He lives in San Diego. San Diego is near the Mexican border.

3. He first got a job as a fruit picker. The job was poorly paid.

4. Jorge learnt English from a friend. His friend's mother was American.

5. Jorge and Ramon now have their own language school. Ramon is from Chile.

Komma oder nicht? 19

11 Höre dir die Sätze an und trage Kommas dort ein, wo sie notwendig sind.

1. Many people who live in California speak Spanish and English.
2. The Spanish which people speak in Mexico is different to the Spanish which people speak in Spain.
3. My friends who are bilingual say Spanish grammar is a little like English grammar.
4. English which was a German language has many words which are like Spanish words because they both come from Latin.

12 *Hollywood.* Ergänze die richtigen Relativpronomen und füge Kommas hinzu, wo nötig.

Hollywood ____ is a part of Los Angeles is known as the centre of the American movie industry. A lot of the industry ____ has grown a lot since it started has moved to neighbouring areas but there are still many old theatres there ____ are used for premieres of shows, for example. Hollywood ____ was then a little village was first used as an area to make films in 1910 by the director D.W. Griffith ____ was actually from New York. The people ____ lived in Hollywood were so friendly that Griffith decided to make lots of other films there. The first movie studio ____ was called Nester Studio was built in Hollywood in 1911 by a company ____ parent company also came from the east of the USA. Since that time many actors and actresses ____ want to become famous have moved to Hollywood.

Partizipien als Adjektive

Das ***present participle*** kennst du von Verlaufsformen. Es ist die *-ing*-Form in den folgenden Sätzen:

I'm **watching** TV.
I was **walking** to school when I saw a famous director.

Das ***past participle*** kennst du von den Perfektformen:
I've never **watched** TV in the morning.
I hadn't **found** my cell phone when you called.

Beide Partizipien können auch als Adjektive verwendet werden. Dabei haben ***present participles*** **aktive** Bedeutung, ***past participles*** **passive** Bedeutung.

The film is **boring.** (der Film langweilt mich → Aktiv)
I'm **bored.** (ich werde gelangweilt → Passiv)
That's an often **asked** question. (die Frage wird oft gestellt → Passiv)
That's an **interesting** question. (es interessiert mich → Aktiv)

13 In Malibu. Vervollständige die Sätze mit dem richtigen als Adjektiv verwendeten Partizip, indem du es aus dem hervorgehobenen Verb bildest.

1. People often see things which **surprise** them in Malibu.

→ People often see ______ things in Malibu. The people are ______

2. Malibu **thrills** people who visit it.

→ There are many ______ visitors in Malibu. Malibu is ______

3. Surfing competitions **excite** people.

→ People watch ______ surfing competitions. The people are

4. But sometimes people see accidents which **shock** them.

→ But sometimes there are ______ accidents. The visitors are

14 Bilde aus dem angegebenen Verb das richtige Adjektiv.

My friend was never the most ____________ (to excite) person around. He was a ____________ (to think) person and so you never found him with the ____________ (to surf) crowd. He was a much ____________ (to love) person because he was very ____________ (to care). He was also a ____________ (to read) person who read any kind of book he found but he wasn't very ____________ (to interest) in the movies. So you can imagine how ____________ (to surprise) I was when he told me that he had got a part in a film. He's a ____________ (to know well) actor now but he hasn't changed at all. He's still quiet.

15 *A bad day?* Übersetze diese Sätze.

1. Was für ein langweiliger Tag!

____

2. Ich langweile mich.

____

3. Heute wird nichts Aufregendes passieren.

____

4. Es gibt keine interessanten Menschen hier.

____

5. Ich bin bekannt und nur an anderen aufregenden Menschen wie mir interessiert.

Lesen: *The Governor of California*

16 Lies den folgenden Text zügig durch, um folgende Fakten zu klären.

1. Who's the Governor of California? ______
2. Where did he come from?
3. What's he best known for? ______
4. When did he start winning bodybuilding competitions? ______

Who would have thought that he would become so famous - the little boy who was born in 1947 in a small Austrian village; the boy who wasn't very good at school, but who did lots of sports and was known as a friendly and happy child? Arnold Schwarzenegger started to make a name for himself as a bodybuilder when he was just 20, but it was only later that he became really famous, as a Hollywood actor in films such as "Terminator" and "Conan the Barbarian". Although he was already rich and famous when he decided to run for *(sich bewerben)* governor of California at the age of 56, not many people expected him to be elected. But he was! Arnie, as some people call him, has managed to do almost everything he has ever wanted to do. So even if you do not like his films or his politics, you should still respect him for that, especially because success didn't come easily to him. He wasn't helped by his family and he didn't have the money to pay for the things he needed; he had to do everything himself.
So how did it all start? When he was a teenager, he played football and one day his trainer took him to a gym. He tried bodybuilding for the first time and he loved it right away. So he started training every day. There are stories that he even broke into the gym at weekends so that he could train when it was closed. Arnold didn't get on with his father or his brother and decided to leave home as soon as possible. Ever since he was young, he had wanted to go to the States because he believed that he could do anything he wanted to do in the US and that he could become rich. He believed that success as a bodybuilder would be his ticket to the States and he was right.
He started winning bodybuilding competitions as a teenager and was invited to live and train in London by a trainer who recognized his talent.
Soon after that, at the age of 20, Arnold became the youngest ever "Mr Universe". He then moved to Munich where he went to business school, worked in a gym and trained over four hours every day. Arnie has always worked hard.
When he was 21, Arnold moved to California. He had already decided that he wanted to become an actor, and that was the best place for him to continue training as a bodybuilder and to try to get a part in a film. Arnold continued to improve as a bodybuilder and became "Mr Olympia" (possibly the most

important bodybuilding title) when he was 23, but it was more difficult for him to become an actor.
One of Arnold's main difficulties in becoming an actor was that he couldn't speak English very well. After a couple of years in the States his English was much better but he still had a very strong accent. Even when he got his first part, in "Hercules in New York" in 1970, another actor had to speak his lines. After that Arnold got parts in more and more successful films. He always played strong men, of course, even when the film was a comedy.
However, it was only in 1982 that he became really successful. He starred in the film "Conan the Barbarian" and it was a hit around the world. Action films were very popular in the 1980s and 1990s and Schwarzenegger had no problem getting parts after "Conan".
Schwarzenegger was very interested in politics and became a Republican as soon as he immigrated to the States. He later used his name and his money to help Republican Presidents, such as Ronald Reagan and George Bush. Although he had never had a job in politics before, he decided to run for governor of California in 2003. And he was elected! The fact that he was famous obviously helped. People have different opinions about the kind of job he did, but enough people were happy to vote for him again in 2006, so that he could stay in office *(Amt)* until 2010.
Schwarzenegger was first successful as a bodybuilder and then became famous by acting in films, but he made his money in business. By the time he was 30 he was a millionaire and that was before he had made any real money in films. He started his first business with a friend, who was also a bodybuilder, in 1968. The business was in building and the earthquake in Los Angeles in 1971 meant that they had a lot of work. He started another business with the money he made from his first one and since that time he has continued to be good at making money.
So what's next for Schwarzenegger? Will he become the first President of the United States not to have been born there?

17 Was hat Schwarzenegger wann gemacht? Ordne den Sätzen Ziffern zu.

- ☐ He moved to Munich.
- ☐ 4 He moved to London.
- ☐ He moved to California.
- ☐ He became "Mr Universe".
- ☐ He became the Governor of California.
- ☐ He started his first business.
- ☐ He acted as "Conan the Barbarian".
- ☐ He became a millionaire.
- ☐ He became "Mr Olympia".

18 Kreuze die richtigen Antworten an. Tipp: Es können mehrere richtig sein!

1. As a child Schwarzegger …

a) was happy. ☐

b) was bad at school. ☐

c) did lots of sports. ☐

2. People first knew Arnold …

a) as a bodybuilder. ☐

b) as an actor. ☐

c) as Governor. ☐

3. He started bodybuilding …

a) when he was a teenager. ☐

b) because he liked it. ☐

c) because he wanted to be rich. ☐

4. He wanted to move to the USA …

a) to become rich. ☐

b) to be free. ☐

c) to escape from his father. ☐

5. He moved to London …

a) because he was invited. ☐

b) so he could learn English. ☐

c) to train as a bodybuilder. ☐

6. In Munich Arnold …

a) worked in a gym. ☐

b) worked in a business school. ☐

c) trained in a gym. ☐

7. Two years after he moved to California …

a) he had become an actor. ☐

b) he had started his first business ☐

c) he had become "Mr Olympia". ☐

8. Schwarzegger acted …

a) once without speaking. ☐

b) in action films. ☐

c) in comedies. ☐

9. As Governor of California …

a) he was liked. ☐

b) he was disliked. ☐

c) he was kind. ☐

10. Arnold became rich by …

a) becoming an actor. ☐

b) bodybuilding. ☐

c) his success in business. ☐

Writing skills: Creative writing

Eine Geschichte schreiben

Wenn du eine Geschichte schreibst, solltest du dir vorher Schauplatz, Handlung und Atmosphäre überlegen.

Schauplatz: Wann und wo passiert die Geschichte? Welche Informationen brauchen die Leser, um sich das vorzustellen?

Handlung: Was passiert in der Geschichte? Wer sind die Hauptpersonen? Was ist der Höhepunkt der Geschichte?

Atmosphäre: Wie sollen sich die Leser fühlen, wenn sie die Geschichte lesen? Wann soll es Spannung geben? Hier helfen Adjektive und Adverbien. Wie ändert sich die Atmosphäre?

Die Geschichte sollte leicht zu lesen sein. Bilde längere Sätze, indem du beispielsweise Relativsätze verwendest, um Zusatzinformationen zu geben, und benütze Konjunktionen, um Gedanken zu verbinden. Kurze Sätze nimmst du, um Spannung einzubauen und eine Tempoänderung vorzunehmen.

19 Lies die folgende Kurzgeschichte. Dann mache dir Notizen zu Schauplatz, Charakteren, Handlung und Atmosphäre.

Janice loved surfing. She was one of the best surfers in her age group in California. She went surfing almost every weekend and so when she started going out with Daniel, who had never been near a surfboard before in his life, one of the first things she did was to teach him how to surf.
He was getting better and better and that Saturday morning he was enjoying it more than ever. Janice was happy watching from the beach because the waves weren't big enough for her that day, so she noticed right away when suddenly everybody started leaving the water. Daniel didn't. He was concentrating on the waves, waiting patiently for a big one. He didn't hear Janice shouting, and he didn't see the shark which was coming towards him. Then he saw it. He started swimming as fast as he could but nobody can out-swim a great white shark. Janice was so scared that no noise would come out of her mouth. She was screaming silently when suddenly Daniel and the surfboard disappeared. She fell down onto the sand and cried. The lifeguards were already going out on their boat, but Janice didn't see them. And she didn't see them coming back again five minutes later with Daniel. He was alive but bleeding a little. She didn't see him until he put his arms around her. They both cried then and only just heard the lifeguard saying, "Sharks don't really like eating people. He probably only just wanted a taste."

Setting: ______________________________

Characters: ______________________________

Plot: ______________________________

____

Atmosphere: ______________________________

20 Lies dir die Vorgaben durch und verfasse daraus eine Kurzgeschichte.

Setting:	highway in south California
Characters:	José (actor), Carla (illegal immigrant)
Plot:	Carla is walking along road. She wants to get a lift to L.A. José passes her in the car and picks her up. He is driving to L.A. Police stop the car. José tells police lies for Carla.
Atmosphere:	thrilling

____

____

____

____

____

____

____

____

____

____

____

Zuhören: *Polite or casual?* 20

21 Höre dir die vier Dialoge an. Ist die Sprache eher höflich oder eher vertraut?

1. ____________; 2. ____________; 3. ____________; 4. ____________

22 Welcher Dialog passt zu welchem Bild?

A. __________; B. __________; C. __________; D. __________

23 In welchen Dialogen hörst du diese Sätze? Trage die richtige Ziffer ein.

Can I get you something? ☐ Can I help you, please? ☐

Oh my God. ☐ Could I speak to Lewis, please? ☐

No, but can you give me a hand with this table? ☐

And do you want him to call you back? ☐

Which beaches would you recommend? ☐

Liz, would you shut up for two seconds. ☐

Could you give him a message for me, please? ☐

And get yourself a drink if you want one. ☐

24 Höre dir die Dialoge nochmals an, dann beantworte die folgenden Fragen.

Dialogue 1

1. Where is Lewis? ______________________

2. When should he be back? ______________________

3. Why won't John be able to go round that night? ______________________

____

4. Should Lewis call John back? ______________________

Dialogue 2

1. What has happened in San Francisco? ______________________

2. Where are Louise and Jane? ______________________

3. Why are they going home early? ______________________

4. When will they get home? ______________________

Dialogue 3

1. How long will the girl be in San Francisco? ______________________

2. What is she interested in? ______________________

3. Why should they wait to hit the beach? ______________________

4. Where are they going next? ______________________

Dialogue 4

1. Why was Kevin early? ______________________

2. What does Tricia want a hand with? ______________________

3. Where are Tricia's parents? ______________________

4. Do they know Tricia is having a big party? ______________________

Lösungen

Zoom-in

1 buildings: flat, house, skyscraper
country: capital, scenery, state
people: cheerleader, immigrant, president

2 across: 4. fireworks; 7. zone
down: 1. energy; 2. journey; 3. classic; 4. freedom; 5. wheat; 6. fee

3 1. true; 2. false; 3. true; 4. true; 5. false; 6. true; 7. false

4 1. Four. 2. USA, US, America, the States. 3. By bus. 4. The Golden Gate Bridge and cable cars. 5. In 1848. 6. Between November and April.

5 Dialogue 1:
Boy: So did you have a good holiday in New York, Mary?
Girl: Yes, it was fantastic. But I didn't just stay in New York, you know.
Boy: Didn't you? But you flew to New York, didn't you?
Girl: Yes, but I had a month's plane ticket. I could fly as much as I wanted to in the States.
Boy: Really? Was it expensive?
Girl: No, it wasn't too expensive. We bought it on the Internet.
Boy: And where did you fly to?
Girl: Well, we spent a week in New York and then we flew to Washington. That was really interesting. Oh, we visited the New England States, too, of course.
Boy: And were they like England?
Girl: No, not really. They were very nice but the best time to visit them is in autumn and people say they are very beautiful then. Anyway, then we flew to Arizona and visited the Grand Canyon.
Boy: Did you fly through it in a helicopter?
Girl: No, we walked through it and stayed there over night. That was great. Then we flew to San Francisco and stayed there for a few days and then we spent our last week on the beach. It was beautiful. I didn't want to come home to London.
Boy: Really. But I'm sure London is much more exciting than the whole of the States, isn't it?
Girl: Yeah, yeah.

→ 3. Notiz: Mary

Dialogue 2:
Girl 1: Hello.
Girl 2: Hi, it's me. I'm sorry I didn't call back earlier. I was on my vacations, you know.
Girl 1: Oh, hi Jill. Did you do the road trip you were talking about?
Girl 2: No, we decided to fly. We only had three weeks and we really wanted to spend some time on the beach.
Girl 1: Did you spend three weeks on the beach then?
Girl 2: No, of course not. We visited Yosemite and drove through Death Valley.
Girl 1: Did you like Yosemite then?
Girl 2: Yeah, it was great but I like Yellowstone National Park better. There are more animals there. I love the coast down there though. We went to a beach near Los Angeles and went swimming every day.
Girl 1: And did you fly to Los Angeles?
Girl 2: No, we flew to San Francisco but we flew back from Los Angeles.

→ 1. Notiz: Jill

Dialogue 3:
Boy: How did you enjoy your road journey? It was your first, wasn't it?
Girl: Well, I did … and I didn't. It's a great feeling when you have driven right across the United States. You kind of feel you know it all, but it's a long way. And sometimes you feel you never want to get in a car again.
Boy: I know how you feel, Cathie. Where did you visit after you left New York?
Girl: We drove to Chicago and visited the Great Lakes, too. Then we drove all the way through the Rocky Mountains and visited Yellowstone National Park. That was something else. I loved it. Then we drove through Nevada – awful place – and finished in San Francisco. Then we sold the car and went surfing for a week.

→ 2. Notiz: Cathie

6

1. Mary flew around the States on her **month's** plane ticket which she bought **on the Internet.** She **walked** through the Grand Canyon. At the end she flew back to **London.**
2. Jill wanted to do a road trip but didn't because she didn't have enough **time.** She liked Yosemite but thought **Yellowstone** was better.
3. Cathie went on her **first** road trip across the States. She loved **Yellow-stone** and they sold the car in San Francisco. She **sometimes** felt that she never wanted to get in a car again.

Unit 1

1 1. elevator; 2. bagel; 3. artist; 4. gate

2 Sandro lives in New York. His parents were **immigrants** from Italy but he was born in America. His **grandparents** still live in Italy and he often goes there. Sandro lives in Little Italy, the Italian part of town, and his **neighbours** speak Italian, too, although the younger people speak English to each other. Last year they moved into a small house with a **yard** behind. It was full of **weeds** and had a small **gate** which didn't lock. Why hadn't the last people looked after it, he wondered. Sandro was trying to get rid of the weeds when a policeman came past and asked, "Did you plant those?" – "What? These weeds?" asked Sandro surprised. The policeman laughed. "They aren't weeds. They're **drugs,**" he said.

3 Glück – happiness; Druck – pressure; Eindruck – impression; Wahl – choice; Mitleid – sympathy; Frieden – peace

4 Jane **did well** at school but she **dropped out** of college because she found it boring. She **said goodbye** to her friends at home and moved to New York. She **looked around** for a job but couldn't find one at first. But then, while she was walking through Manhattan, she **happened to** see an ad in the window of a diner. She went in to ask for the job but the diner was full. After some time she **noticed** that only one person was working there and he was tired out. She watched for some time and saw how things were done. Then she **pushed** her way through the crowd, went behind the counter and **served** for the rest of the day. She was serving one customer when she suddenly **recognized** him. It was a famous actor. But it couldn't be him, could it? Yes, this was New York and anything was possible.

5
1. You need a lot of **luck** to win 1000 dollars. I won it but I was **unlucky** because I lost it before I spent it.
2. I love skateboarding but I'm **hopeless** at it. **Hopefully** I'll learn something at the skateboard park this afternoon.
3. There are still many **immigrants** in New York but there is not as much **immigration** now.
4. She has been very **happy** since she met him and you can see her **happiness** in her smile.

6 1. “I came in here **ages ago** and I still haven’t been served.”
2. “I’m too small. Nobody can see me **at the back of** the queue.”
3. “This place is always full. There’s a queue **at any time** of day.”
4. “I’ve been waiting **for** ages.”
5. “Two bagels and a coffee to go?” – “**Over here,** please.”
6. “I love this place. I’ve been coming here **since** I was six.”

7 1. I enjoyed the party **very much.**
2. I **really** loved the music.
3. The food was **extremely/really** delicious.
4. I met a girl there who was **pretty/very** exciting.
5. But she was **completely** hopeless at dancing.
6. But I **quite** enjoyed meeting her.
7. Unfortunately I **completely** forgot that my girlfriend was there, too.

8 That food tastes very, very good. It’s **delicious.**
He really wants to be best at everything. He’s very **ambitious.**
I love painting pictures, but I’m really bad at it. I’m **hopeless.**
She never works at anything. She’s very **lazy.**
The garden was all weeds last year and it’s beautiful now. That’s **amazing.**
That book is difficult to read because the language is so **colloquial.**
I fell off my chair. It was very **embarrassing.**

9 1. underground – subway; 2. taxi – cab; 3. holiday – vacation; 4. city centre – downtown; 5. flat – apartment; 6. sweets – candy; 7. storey – story; 8. programme – program; 9. neighbourhood – neighborhood; 10. theatre – theater; 11. bill – check; 12. rubbish – trash; 13. toilet – restroom; 14. trousers – pants

10 1. I’ve got so much work at school but I really need to help the guys with the mural. – I **wish** I **could help** but I’m terrible at painting.
2. My cousins are coming again this summer from England. – Oh, great. **I’m really looking forward** to meeting them.
3. My dad had a car crash and he’s in hospital now. I’m very worried about him. – **How terrible!**
4. Guess what! I’ve won the mural competition. I’m going to meet some top mural artists next week. – **That’s amazing!** – Yes, **it’s too brilliant for words.**

11 John **arrived** in New York yesterday. He **has never been** to America before, so he’s very excited. He’s staying with his girlfriend, Janet. She**’s lived** in New York for six months and **hasn’t seen** everything yet. They**’ve just taken** an elevator to the top of the Empire State Building. Jane **has been** up before but the weather **wasn’t** very good then so she couldn’t see much. Today the view is excellent and they can see the whole of New York, but, oh no, John **has forgotten** his camera.

12 1. John **has been working** since 8 am.
2. Ella **has been eating** her lunch for an hour.
3. I **have been waiting** for lunch for twenty minutes.
4. Dave and Alice **have been having** an argument since 11:00.

13 1. Alice has been playing the guitar since eight o'clock.
2. John has been drawing since he arrived.

14 1. Miguel has been working for seven hours.
2. Tina and her friends have been dancing since half past ten.

15 I **have been working** in this diner **since** I **came** to New York two years ago. I **have served** thousands of customers and I know some of them quite well. Some **have been coming** in here **since** I **started** to work here.
There's old Antonia. She **has been living** in New York **for** sixty-five years and she still speaks Italian better than English. Then there's Chan. He **has tried** every single sandwich and bagel we have in here and often gives us new ideas. And then there's William. He **has been coming** here **since** my boss **opened** the café and he **has never paid** for a bagel once. But then as my boss **has often said** dogs don't need to pay.

16 The garden looked wonderful. It **had been** hard work but it was worth it. It **had taken** over a year to finish, but the garden **was** now a nice place to relax in. First they **had taken** out the weeds and then they **had planted** some trees. It **had been** fun and now it was finished so they **wanted** to have a big party to show everybody what they **had done.** The party was on Saturday and they were all very excited when they **arrived.** But when they **went** in, they got a shock. Somebody **had pulled** lots of flowers out of the ground. They were angry. Who **had done** it? Then they found out. Two foxes **had moved** into the garden over night. "Well, we wanted to share our garden," laughed Marie.

17 Alice **had been cleaning** the diner for an hour when some friends arrived. They **had been shopping** since the shops **opened.** When everything was ready, Alice and her friends **had been preparing** food for an hour. When Diego **arrived** at his diner, everybody **had been hiding** under the tables for a few minutes. When everybody **shouted**, "Happy Birthday Diego", he **had been wondering** where everybody was.

18 1. Mac and his brother had been watching films all night.
2. A man had been cleaning windows since 7 o'clock.

19 1. I had been jogging for half an hour when I saw a famous actor.
2. Jenny had been looking for the zoo for ages before she found it.
3. You had been reading a book when it started to rain.

20 I love to see almost everybody happy.
I find the people friendly.
The subway makes me nervous.
We like the streets full of people.

21 1. The smell of the food always makes me hungry.
2. They always cook their food fresh.
3. The boss likes to keep the guests happy.

22 New York is an **exciting** place and some people call it **beautiful.** A lot of people live and work in a very **small** area so the streets and shops are often **full.** But you can do anything in New York: skate **fast** in Central Park or sail **slowly** in the harbour. You can eat **well** in one of the thousands of restaurants or eat **cheaply** in a diner. But there's maybe one thing you can't do in New York: get **bored!**

23 1. (abgeschwächt) It's quite/pretty nice.
(verstärkt) It's very/really nice.
(weiter verstärkt) It's extremely nice.
2. (abgeschwächt) I quite like it./I like it a bit.
(verstärkt) I like it very much/a lot./I really like it.
3. (abgeschwächt) She sings quite/pretty well.
(verstärkt) She sings very/really well.
(weiter verstärkt) She sings extremely well.
4. (abgeschwächt) I've almost finished.
(verstärkt) I've completely finished./I've finished completely.

24 1. Many people eat **in diners.** → adverbial of place
2. You can **easily** find your way around New York. → adverb of manner
3. We've **always** lived in Little Italy. → adverb of frequency
4. Times Square is busy **at night.** → adverbial of time

25 1. Mustafa was born in Germany in 1991./In 1991 Mustafa was born in Germany.
2. He had always been interested in the States.
3. He moved to the US in 2009./In 2009 he moved to the US.

4. He didn't speak English very well at first./At first he didn't speak English very well.
5. Mustafa has happily lived/has lived happily in New York since July last year./Since July last year Mustafa has happily lived/has lived happily in New York.

26 I work in a diner.
I work in a diner on Saturdays.
I work happily in a diner on Saturdays.
I work happily in a diner at lunchtime on Saturdays.
I work happily in a diner in New York at lunchtime on Saturdays.
I often work happily in a diner in New York at lunchtime on Saturdays.

27 I **live** in Little Italy and I work in an Italian restaurant. My parents are Italian and I **look** Italian but I **don't speak** Italian. This is a problem because guests often **come** in and speak to me in Italian and I **don't understand** a word. My boss is American, but he **speaks** Italian. He **feels** Italian he says. "What **does it feel** like?" I ask but he **doesn't reply.**
I've decided to learn Italian and so now **I'm staying** at my grandparents' house near Rome. **I'm trying** to cross a road now. Everybody **is driving** past me and I can't cross. These Italians are crazy. Teenagers **drive** their mopeds in and out of the traffic. Why **don't they crash?** A woman **comes** and crosses the road before me. She just **walks** into the road and the cars drive around her. These Italians are crazy and I love them.

28 New York is very big and yesterday I was glad because I **wanted** some time alone to think about the future. But then I **was walking** through Central Park when I met a friend, Zak. He **had just met** another friend of ours, Pamela. Pamela **had been skating** all morning around the park but I hadn't seen her. Zak and I were talking when we **saw** Gina, too. Gina **was looking** for Pamela but couldn't find her. **I've been living** in New York for two years and I've never met anybody I know by chance. So why **was everybody** in Central Park that day? Then I found out. There was a free concert with lots of stars that afternoon.

29
1. What food should we buy? – Well, we**'re going to make** a big pizza. – OK. I**'ll get** some cheese and tomatoes.
2. Do you think we should eat outside? – No, I think it**'ll be** too cold.
3. Where's Henry? Isn't he coming? – Yes, but his train **doesn't arrive** until half past six. – Oh, he**'ll have arrived** then by now. It's already six forty.

30 a), c), e), h), i), j), l)

31 This time tomorrow I'**ll have left** New York. I will be on a plane back to England. I'**ve had** a great time here and it's funny to think I **hadn't wanted** to come here at all. I only **came** because my best friend had immigrated to New York the summer before. She **loves** it here and I think she'**ll never leave**. And me? I'**m going to live** here one day, too.

32 a) 2.; b) 5.; c) 4.; d) 1.; e) 3.

33 1. In New York. 2. In 1930. 3. In England. 4. The roof fell down. 5. Until he was 13. 6. To go back to New York. 7. 19. 8. English.

34 1. true; 2. not in the text; 3. true; 4. false; 5. true; 6. true; 7. false; 8. not in the text

Korrektur:

4. The church gave money to Angela.
7. Frank had three brothers when he sailed back to New York.

35

1. Frank wanted to burn some wood to **keep warm.**
2. Frank wrote some letter to try and make **people scared.**
3. Frank found New York **exciting.**
4. He **had been working** for a few years when he paid for his family to join him in New York.

36

1. I don't believe …/I really don't think …/If you ask me, …
2. Personally, I find …
3. In my opinion/I believe …

37 *Lösungsvorschlag:* I believe that everybody would steal if they were hungry enough. I think it's difficult to talk about right and wrong when people are so poor. If you ask me, it's wrong that they were so poor. In my opinion the money lender was wrong. She was rich but she didn't help the poor people.

38 Dialogue 1:

Woman: Excuse me!
Waiter: Just a moment!

Dialogue 2:

Waiter: OK. Whose is this bagel?
Man: Over here, please. It's mine.

Dialogue 3:

Man: I'd like a coffee to go and …
Woman: Hey, it's my turn! I've been waiting for ages.
Man: No, that isn't true …

Dialogue 4:
Woman: Could you please help me?
Waiter: I'm sorry, but all these people are before you.

Dialogue 5:
Man: I'd like to order, please.
Woman: Everybody would like to order.
Waiter: I'm very sorry but my assistant is ill today.

1. Excuse me!
2. Over here, please.
3. Hey, it's my turn!
4. Could you please help me?
5. I'd like to order, please.

39

1. **BE:** Could you give me a bagel, please?
2. **AE:** Could you gimme a bagel, please?
3. **AE:** I ain't really hungry.
4. **BE:** I'm not really hungry.
5. **BE:** A bagel is a kind of bread roll.
6. **AE:** A bagel is a kinda bread roll.
7. **AE:** It's half after five. What time's she gonna come?
8. **BE:** It's half five. What time is she going to come?
9. **AE:** I dunno where she is but I gotta go now.
10. **BE:** I don't know where she is but I've got to go now.

40

1. Could you gimme a bagel, please?
2. I ain't really hungry.
3. A bagel is a kinda bread roll.
4. It's half after five. What time's she gonna come?
5. I dunno where she is but I gotta go now.

41

Dialogue 1:
Boy: Excuse me. Could you tell me if there is anywhere that's good to eat around here?
Woman: Oh yeah. There's the most wonderful diner around the corner. They make the most delicious bagels and it isn't at all expensive. Or if you like Chinese food, there's a great restaurant downtown. It isn't far. Or you can take the subway – it's just one stop. But if you haven't got a ticket then you can walk …

Dialogue 2:
Boy: Excuse me. I'm looking for a diner. I think it's just near here.
Man: Oh, you probably mean the Hollywood Diner. Yes, it's not far from here. It's in West 16th Street, so it's easy to find. We're in Christopher

Street. So you go down here until you get to 6th Road. Turn left and just keep going until you get to 16th Street West. Turn right there and it's just on your left.

Dialogue 3:

Man: Next please.

Boy: Hello. I'd like a coffee to go, and what kind of sandwiches have you got, please?

Man: We've got cheese, chicken, cheese and vegetables, salami, pastrami, bacon ...

1. e); 2. c); 3. b)

42 *Dialogfortsetzung zu* 1.:

Boy: Excuse me. I'm very sorry but my English isn't very good. Do you think you could speak more slowly, please?

Woman: Oh, I'm very sorry. Yes, well. There's the most wonderful diner around the corner. They make delicious bagels and it isn't expensive. Or do you like Chinese food?

Boy: Yes.

Woman: Well, there's a great restaurant downtown. It isn't far. Or you can take the subway – it's just one stop.

Dialogfortsetzung zu 2.:

Boy: I'm sorry. I didn't understand you. Could you repeat that, please?

Man: Oh, yes, of course, sorry. Well, we're in Christopher Street. You go down here until you get to 6th Road. Turn left and just keep going until you get to 16th Street West. Turn right there and it's just on your left.

Boy: Oh, thanks very much. That sounds easy.

Dialogfortsetzung zu 3.:

Boy: I'm sorry. What is a pastrami, please?

Man: Pastrami? That's a kind of spicy beef. Meat, you know.

Boy: Oh, well, I'd like cheese and bacon, please.

Man: OK. Coming up.

1. a wonderful diner or a Chinese restaurant; 2. 16th Street West; 3. 6th Road; 4. coffee to go and a cheese and bacon sandwich

Revision A (Unit 1)

1 New York gets a present → E.
New York becomes English → A.
A difficult time for immigrants → D.
New York becomes a city → F.
Immigration stations → C.
The first American President → B.

2 3 – 10 – 8 – 5 – 7 – 9 – 6 – 11 – 1 – 4 – 2

3 1. false; 2. not in the text; 3. true; 4. false; 5. false; 6. true

4
1. Native Americans lived in New York before the Europeans arrived.
4. The first immigrant who arrived at Ellis Island was a girl from Ireland.
5. The Statue of Liberty is on Liberty Island.

5
1. The English **fought** the Dutch in 1664, **took** New Amsterdam and then **called** it New York.
2. Immigrants **had landed** in Manhattan **before** the immigration station on Ellis Island was opened.
3. The number of people in New York **grew from** 1700 until 1898.
4. Immigrants have moved to New York **for** almost 400 years.

6 Dialogue 1:
Girl: Who's next?
Man: Me, I think.
Girl: What can I get you?
Man: I'd like two coffees to go, a cheese bagel and a bacon and egg sandwich, please.
Girl: OK. Two coffees, one cheese bagel and one bacon and egg sandwich. That's twelve dollars sixty.
Man: Here you are.
Girl: Thanks.

Dialogue 2:
Woman: We'd like to order, please.
Girl: Yes, what would you like?
Woman: Well, do you do a breakfast menu?

Girl: Yes, we do a special for ten dollars. That's one coffee, one bottle of water, bacon and eggs, two pieces of toast or a bagel.
Woman: OK. Then we'd like two special breakfasts please.
Girl: With toast or a bagel?
Woman: With bagels please.
Girl: OK. That's twenty dollars, please.

1. Two coffees to go, one cheese bagel and one bacon and egg sandwich.
2. Twelve dollars sixty.
3. One coffee, one bottle of water, bacon and eggs, two pieces of toast or a bagel.
4. Two special breakfasts with bagels.
5. Twenty dollars.

7 Dear Mum,
I'm having a great time here in New York. I arrived on Thursday and I've been staying in a great hostel in Greenwich Village. I met some great guys at the hostel and we've visited Chinatown and the Empire State Building together. I've been sitting in Central Park all day today and just watching the people. It's great.
Yours,
Dan

8
1. Yes. I'm really enjoying it here in New York./Yes, I like it./Yes, it's great.
2. I'm really looking forward to visiting the Statue of Liberty./I'm really excited about seeing the Statue of Liberty.
3. That's amazing./That's great./Fantastic.
4. How terrible!/That's very sad.

9 *Oma:* Frag ihn, ob es irgendwo hier in der Gegend etwas Gutes zu essen gibt.
Du: **Is there anywhere good to eat around here?**
Mann: Yes, there's a great diner around the corner. It sells delicious bagels.
Du: **Um die Ecke gibt es ein tolles Schnellrestaurant mit leckeren Bageln.**
Oma: Schön. Frag ihn noch, ob man leicht zum Zentrum kommt.
Du: **And is it easy to go downtown from here?**
Mann: Well, downtown Manhattan isn't far. You can walk or take the subway.
Du: **Es ist nicht weit – wir können laufen oder mit der U-Bahn fahren.**

Unit 2

1

e	a	u	**t**	**d**	**u**	**d**	**e**	**a**
f	c	q	**e**	z	j	i	s	**d**
h	t	a	**e**	n	**g**	u	x	**u**
p	**r**	**i**	**n**	**c**	**i**	**p**	**a**	**l**
b	o	k	s	y	**r**	d	p	**t**
n	n	e	a	m	**l**	o	c	k
l	s	c	**a**	**u**	**t**	**h**	**o**	**r**

1. Students sometimes have to see the **principal.**
2. He isn't a child, he's an **adult.**
3. Nicola isn't a guy, she's a **girl.**
4. Who's the **author** of that book?
5. Who's Kyle? Is he that cool **dude** over there?
6. Are you a **teen** but not yet 18? Do you want a job?

2 So you wanted to know about my school here in New York State? Well! We have eight **periods** a day and the first one usually starts at 8.30. If you are late for school or for **classes,** you get **detention** after school. We have three **semesters** every year. I'm in the 8th **grade** and I love it. And why? Because I'm a cheerleader now and so I can do extra **gymnastics** every week and choose a boyfriend from the football team!

3 If you want to go into **politics,** you must enjoy debating important subjects. You don't need any special **qualifications** but you must know and care about the **laws** in your country. It is an **advantage** if you can talk well because you must be able to convince people that your ideas are good. You need to be able to present your arguments well and be able to explain all the important **points** both for and against. You have to enjoy **discussions** and you will have a big **disadvantage** if you cannot listen to people.

4 1. auschecken; 2. wählen; 3. verpasste; 4. präsentierte; 5. mogelte; 6. üben; 7. griff (nach)/packte

5 **To present arguments:** As you can see, …; It's obvious that …
To agree: I agree with you. I think you're right.
To disagree: I see what you mean, but …; That's true, but …

6 I think we should play more soccer in the US and less football. And why? **First,** I think soccer is more important **because** it is played all over the world. Every four years the football world championship is played with countries from all over the world. We play, too, **but** the US never does well. **Next,** sport is important in the US, **but** most sports which we play are only played in a few countries, **so** we usually win. **For example,** baseball and American football are not played in many other countries at all. I think when more people play a sport, the level at which the sport is played gets higher. **That is why** I think we should play a world sport like soccer in the US and not just an American sport. **Finally,** I think soccer is much more fun.

7 autumn → fall; class/year → grade; colour → color; favourite → favorite; jewellery → jewelry; lesson → class; mobile → cell phone; Mum → Mom; to organise → to organize; to practise → to practice

8 angry – furious; last – final; clear – obvious; not open – closed; great – brilliant; tasty – delicious

9 1. Neil and Billy might have met in town by chance.
2. They must have had a good time at the diner.
3. Neil can't have split up from his girlfriend.
4. So he shouldn't have asked Billy to the dance.

10 1. Chan might have enjoyed the dance.
2. He must have liked me or he wouldn't have asked me.
3. I shouldn't have talked to Kate so much.
4. I could have danced with Chan more.
5. I needn't have worried about another date.

11 1. The try-outs must have started early. I'm sure I wasn't late.
2. I should have practiced more before.
3. She could have given me another chance.
4. I needn't have gone at all.

12 We don't have a school uniform, but blue pullovers, trousers and skirts **must be worn.** Dresses **can be worn,** too. Mobile phones **may be taken** to school but they **must not be used** in school. MP3 players **cannot be taken** to school because they are not needed. Sandwiches **needn't be taken** to school because school dinners **can be bought** in the cafeteria. If you are ill, a note **must be brought** from your parents.

13
1. Young people expect to be given good jobs without working.
2. They want to be paid even when they don't work.
3. They hope to be discovered in stupid television programmes.
4. My grandson says young people would like to be understood by us old folk.

14
1. Teachers want to be treated with respect.
2. Students expect to be taught well by teachers.
3. Bikes can be left in the sheds.
4. School uniforms must be worn by students.
5. Parents would like to be informed about their kids by the teachers.

15
Girls! So you **want to be invited** to the ball? Wake up! We're living in the 21st century – now boys **can be asked** by you. But first a boy **must be found.** And first you must decide what you want. Do you want to dance at the ball? If you are lucky, good dancers **may be found** at a dancing lesson. What? You just want a cool dude? Sorry! It **has to be said:** they aren't easy to find!
Boys! So you **expect to be asked** to the ball by a 21st century girl? Dream on! Good luck **must be created** first.

16
1. F.; 2. B.; 3. C.; 4. A.; 5. D.; 6. E.

17
a), c) und d)

18
1. false; 2. true; 3. true; 4. true; 5. false; 6. true; 7. true; 8. false
Korrektur:
1. Some school uniforms are just black trousers and pullover, for example.
5. It's an advantage.
8. Differences should be respected.

19
1. Z. 4–5 (… when firms only make a small number of trousers, for example, they are always more expensive than when they make a large number.)
2. Z. 8–10 (At times when pupils are growing fast, this can mean that parents have to buy two school uniforms in a year and two lots of normal clothes, too.)
3. Z. 41–43 (I think pupils should learn to respect each other's differences at school and not learn how to hide them.)

20
A new friend

21 1. a); 2. a), c); 3. b); 4. c); 5. a), b)

22 1. disadvantage; 2. not important; 3. advantage; 4. advantage; 5. advantage; 6. disadvantage; 7. advantage; 7. not important

23 *Lösungsvorschlag:* Student councils are necessary in schools. They organise events and give teachers the students' opinions.
The main advantage of being a member of the council is that you can change things at school. You can make school like you want it to be.
Other advantages are that you can have fun and make new friends there.
You can also find out new things.
The main disadvantage is that meetings take lots of time and you have less time to do other things.
Another disadvantage is that meetings can be boring.
In my opinion there are more advantages of being a member of the council but obviously you have to be the kind of person who likes to discuss things.

24
Mr Elliot: OK. Is there anything else?
Jed: Yes, er, we think MP3 players should be allowed in schools.
Mrs Jefferies: Well, I'm sorry but we've spoken about it many times and all the teachers think …
Mr Elliot: (clears his throat)
Mrs Jefferies: … almost all the teachers agree that we have too many problems when there are MP3 players in school.
Jed: There are problems with lots of things but we're still allowed to bring them.
Mrs Jefferies: Like what, for example?
Jill: Like bikes, cell phones …
Mrs Jefferies: Yes, you're right. We have problems with those things but there are more advantages than disadvantages when students bring them. There are no real advantages to MP3 players.
Jed: I'm afraid I don't agree. Music has lots of advantages. It makes you feel good. Er …
Mr Elliot: And I'm sure you will agree that music helps you think.
Mrs Jefferies: You may be right. Some kinds of music help you think, but the kind of music most students listen to makes them aggressive.
Jed: I'm sorry, I disagree and I don't think that's fair.
Mrs Jefferies: OK, but it's obvious there are just too many problems with MP3 players. Students lose them. They are stolen. Students listen to them in lessons. Students listen to them and don't talk to their friends.
Mr Elliot: But students listen to them with their friends, too. They talk about music and not just about football or TV.

Jill:	Yes. And I'd like to make another point. Now you can listen to music on most cell phones and cell phones are allowed in school. It's just students who are very interested in music and want to listen to it on high quality MP3 players who are not allowed to.
Mr Elliot:	Yes, I agree with you, Jill, and I think we'll have to talk about it in our next teacher's meeting. Don't you agree, Mrs Jefferies?
Mrs Jefferies:	Yes, Mr Elliot. We'll have to talk about it in the teacher's meeting with the other teachers who don't teach music.
Jed:	Thank you, Mr Elliot.

Arguments for MP3 players in school:
1. Music makes people feel good.
2. Music helps you think.
3. Students listen together and talk about music.
4. You can listen to music on cell phones anyway.

Arguments against MP3 players in school:
1. Music can make people feel aggressive.
2. Students lose them.
3. MP3 players are stolen.
4. Students listen to them in lessons.
5. Students listen to them and don't talk to their friends.

25 **To present arguments:** And I'm sure you will agree that …/… it's obvious …/And I'd like to make another point.
To agree: Yes, you're right./You may be right./Yes, I agree with you.
To disagree: I'm afraid I don't agree./I'm sorry, I disagree.

26 1. cell phones and bikes; 2. football and TV; 3. in the teacher's meeting; 4. music

27
1. Yes, you're right./Yes, I agree./Yes, that's right.
2. I'm afraid I don't agree./I'm sorry, I don't agree./That's not true./That isn't right.
3. You may be right./That may be true./That could be true./You're probably right.
4. I'm sorry, I disagree./I'm afraid I disagree./I'm sorry, I don't think you're right.
5. Yes, I agree with you./Yes, you're right./Yes, that's right.

Unit 3

1 1. a) gas station; b) cashier
2. a) canyon; b) sunset; c) covered wagon

2 natural: The Grand Canyon was formed by **nature.**
real: There are great photos of it, but none of them come near to **reality.**
beautiful: You can see the whole **beauty** of the area from the Skywalk.
explain: It's difficult to believe the **explanation** of how the canyon was formed.
like: It doesn't matter what your **likes** and dislikes are, you'll like it here.

3 1. suburb; 2. **c**ouple; 3. **r**eser**va**tion; 4. settl**e**r; 5. **m**ember; 6. e**n**viro**n**ment;
7. tr**i**b**e**; 8. st**a**te; 9. journ**alist**
A person who lived in the US before white people arrived: **Native American**

4 1. Mexico (this is a country); 2. Scot (this is a person, the others are nationalities or adjectives); 3. the American (this is just one person);
4. dude (this is just one person)

5 to keep – halten; to point – zeigen; to mix – mischen; to develop – entwickeln; to admire –bewundern; to portray – darstellen;
to experience – erfahren

6 I've always dreamt **of** going skiing, but I never thought I'd be able to because it's so expensive. When two friends started talking **about** a skiing holiday, I let them talk. They'd often organised things and I'd got excited but then they'd let me **down.** But then they said there was a school trip to the slopes. "Come **along** to the meeting," they said.
I went. I was afraid **of** it being very expensive and it was, but this time I really felt **like** a holiday, so I decided to get a job and pay for myself. I looked **for** a job and found one. I looked forward **to** the skiing holiday all winter but even when I got **on** the bus to the mountains in February, I couldn't believe that I was really going. We got there and I loved it. I wasn't good **at** skiing but I loved the beautiful environment, and I think even if I lived there, I'd never get tired **of** the beautiful views and the snow.

7 I'm not joking. I'm **serious.**
That's a **low** bridge, isn't it? Can big ships go under there?
Is the Loch Ness Monster real? Or is it a **mythical** animal?
I didn't expect that at all. That's very **surprising.**
The view is amazing. It's **breathtaking.**
The Grand Canyon is **natural.** People didn't make it.
The Grand Canyon is very long. It's **huge.**
She's always **relaxed.** Nothing much worries her at all.
Tastes are different. What one person thinks is beautiful, the other thinks is **ugly.**

8 to practise → to practice
travelling → traveling
motorway → highway
trousers → pants
railway → railroad
jewellery → jewelry

9 1. Excuse me for asking, but are you from Texas?
2. Would you recommend seeing the Skywalk?
3. I just love hitting the slopes.
4. The people here are very nice.
5. You're right about that.
6. Excuse me, could you take a picture of us, please?
7. Have a great vacation!
8. I'm sorry, but I don't agree.
9. Nice to meet you.
10. I'd be happy to, no problem.
11. The open spaces here are fantastic.
12. It was really nice to have met you.

10 Starting a conversation: 1., 6., 9.
Continuing a conversation: 2., 3., 4., 11.
Finishing a conversation: 7., 12.
Disagreeing: 8.
Agreeing: 5.
Replying to a question: 10.

11 I'd visit my friend in the mountains and go skiing this weekend if I **had** a car. I don't have much money. If I **had** enough money, **I'd buy** a car. I'm looking for a job. If I **find** one, **I'll buy** my own car in a few months. If I **don't find** a job quickly, I **won't be able to** go skiing this winter again. But I'm lucky: if I **hadn't got** my driver's license last June, I **wouldn't have been able to** go skiing last month. But then if I **hadn't had** an accident in my mum's car, she **would have lent** me hers.

12 I love **lying** in bed and **getting up** late at the weekend, so last weekend when the phone rang at 10 am, I was still lying in bed. It was a new friend. She wanted to know if I liked **skiing** and if I wanted to go to the mountains with her. I lay there and imagined **skiing** down a mountain. It was beautiful. **Listening** to great music in a car while you are driving through beautiful countryside is wonderful, too. I wanted to go but an hour later she was sitting in her car and driving to the Rockies and I was still lying in bed. I can't ski! I'm going to start **learning.** Tomorrow!
(die anderen -ing-Formen sind Teil einer present-progressive-Form)

13
1. I love living in Montana.
2. Tomorrow I'm going to start learning to ride a horse.
3. I can imagine going to school on my horse.
4. Driving a car is boring.

14
1. I'd often imagined living in California.
2. I love swimming in the sea and surfing.
3. Living in Kansas is not very exciting.
4. I didn't think I would mind moving house.
5. But leaving your friends is much more difficult than I expected.

15
1. What are you looking forward to doing in your holidays?
2. We are talking about visiting California.
3. I am interested in driving along Route 66.
4. We are worried about getting bored in the car.

16 I've always dreamt of **going** to the Rockies. I've imagined **walking** through the mountains and **sleeping** under the clear sky. I've always been crazy about **watching** animals in their own environment. Now my dream has come true and it's as beautiful and exciting as I imagined. Now I'm sitting by a river and watching fish jump out. Wild cats are watching them, too. It's great and I could stay here forever. I'm not looking forward to **going** home back to my city life again.

17 My children keep telling me I should ~~doing~~ → **do** more sport but it's more difficult than they think. I don't like ~~jog~~ → **to jog/jogging** and I can't get used to ~~go~~ → **going** to the gym. I love to cycle, but the last time I was ~~rideing~~ → **riding** my bike into town, a car almost hit me. I love skiing but obviously you can only ~~doing~~ → **do** that in winter. One of my favorite hobbies is ~~swiming~~ → **swimming** in the sea but we live in Texas so I can't do that very often. I stopped ~~do~~ → **doing** gymnastics when I stopped being a cheerleader. I'd like ~~trying~~ → **to try** in-line skating but I'm scared of ~~break~~ → **breaking** my leg. I'm very interested in rock climbing and I could ~~practising~~ → **practise** on a climbing wall in the gym but I don't want to risk ~~haveing~~ → **having** an accident. I like football but I'm not very good at ~~play~~ → **playing** with balls, so I'll just have to keep watching it on TV!

18 I am tired of my sister wearing my clothes.
I don't like my parents arguing.
They aren't too happy about us fighting.

19 1. his dad; 2. his friends; 3. Nick/himself; 4. Californians; 5. Nick/himself; 6. his new classmates; 7. Nick/himself

20
1. I'm very excited about becoming a cheerleader.
2. I like my friends watching the training.
3. I'm a bit nervous about making a mistake at a match.
4. I'm worried about the fans laughing at me.
5. I'm looking forward to having a date with a footballer.

21
1. The job hadn't been advertised for long.
2. My parents had to be asked before everything could be agreed.
3. The museum will be opened tomorrow.
4. The Native American lifestyle is often not understood very well.
5. I have been offered a job in a new museum about Native Americans./ A job in a new museum about Native Americans has been offered to me.

22 Native Americans **have not always been treated** badly by Europeans since the two peoples met. When the first villages **were founded** by white settlers, Native Americans and Europeans often **tried** to talk to each other. Settlers were helped by the Americans when they **had/were having** problems to find enough food. Native Americans, of course, didn't need **to be helped** by the settlers.
Later, as more and more Europeans **arrived** and more and more land **was needed,** Native Americans **were pushed** off their land. If they did not go, they **were killed.** Land that **had been used** by the Americans for thousands of years was quickly taken from them. In the 19th century reservations **were created** for Native Americans. Native Americans **didn't have** any choice. Now Native Americans and their lifestyle **are usually respected** by Europeans. Native Americans must **be treated** the same as all other Americans but, of course, their lifestyle **has been changed** for ever. The land cannot **be used** as it once was.

23
1. The Skywalk was being built when I first visited the Grand Canyon.
2. Lots of articles were being written about it at that time.
3. Not as many negative articles are being written about it now.

24 1. The café was (just) being opened when I arrived.
2. Bagels were being prepared.
3. The tables were being laid when I walked into the café.
4. The food/My bagel is being served while I am reading my magazine.

25 Some jewelry **was stolen** at school on Monday and when I arrived yesterday questions **were being asked** by the police. The burglar **was never caught** but some of the things **were found** in a bird's nest a week later.

26 1. The Grand Canyon was carved out by the Colorado River.
2. The land was lived on by tribes of Native Americans before Europeans moved there.
3. The environment is looked after by the National Park.
4. The land has not been built on much by developers.
5. The canyon has been flown over and driven through.
6. It must have been dreamt about by anybody who has seen it once.

27 1. a) Pronomen/Subjekt, b) Adjektiv, c) *gerund*/Objekt
2. a) Nomen/Subjekt, b) Possessivbegleiter/Objekt, c) Objekt/*-ing*-Form
3. a) Nomen/Subjekt, b) *past participle* (Teil des Verbs), c) adverbiale Bestimmung des Ortes

Vorschläge:
1. **They** have always been **bad** at **drawing.**
2. My **friends** are worried about **us** not **feeling** well at school.
3. **Beers** were being **drunk** as I arrived **at the bar.**

28 Zusammenfassung **b)** passt am besten.

29 **Story in the film:** She's a Native American and he's a white American. The American Government want the Navajo to move to a reservation. They fight and soldiers hurt and catch the chief. The hero rescues him. At the end the hero and the woman kiss.
The story of making the film: She's a Native American and he's a white American. She doesn't like the hero. They film together but she doesn't talk to him. They have an interview with a journalist. She starts to understand the hero.

30 1. line 5; 2. line 7/8; 3. line 9/10; 4. line 37/38; 5. line 43–45; 6. line 54; 7. line 56/57; 8. line 67–68; 9. line 76

31 1. He must have been in pain but John could not see any signs of it in his face. (l. 3–4)
2. The sun was going down as John and Chief … (l. 11)

3. … and she sounded so serious. (l. 53)
4. … she could not stop herself from smiling back again. (l. 74–75)

32 Dialogue 1:

Woman: Hello.
Man: Good morning. Nice day today, isn't it?
Woman: Yes. Are you having a party today?
Man: Yes. How can you tell?
Woman: Well. That looks like party food to me.
Man: Yes, you're right. I've just got a new job so I'm throwing a party for a few friends.
Woman: Great. I hope you'll be very happy and very rich.
Man: Thank you very much.
Woman: That's OK. Have a nice day.

Dialogue 2:

Woman: Oh, I'm very sorry. Did I stand on your toe?
Man: No, not all. Don't worry. I was standing in the way.
Woman: Excuse me for asking, but are you from England?
Man: Yes, I am. How could you tell?
Woman: That's your cute accent. I just love an English accent. You hear it in the movies sometimes.
Man: Well, thank you.
Woman: So where are you from in England?
Man: I'm from London but I've been living here in the States for a year.
Woman: You don't say! And do you like it here?
Man: Yes, I love it. It's a beautiful place and the people are so friendly.
Woman: Well. Thank you.
Man: And I think the skiing is probably the best in the world.
Woman: Well, enjoy yourself while you're here.
Man: Thank you. It was really nice to have met you.

Dialogue 3:

Woman: Do you mind if I sit here?
Man: No, not at all. Here, I'll move my coat.
Woman: Wow. What a great view!
Man: Yeah, it's really something, ain't it? But you're not from around here, are you?
Woman: No, I'm not.
Man: May I ask you where you're from?
Woman: I'm from New York. I'm just out here on holiday.
Man: And do you like it?
Woman: Well, I only arrived yesterday so I haven't seen a lot, but I love what I've seen. Are you from around here?
Man: Well, I'm from Los Angeles but I'm living in Jackson so I know it quite well now.

Woman: And what would you recommend doing while I'm here?
Man: Well, have you ever been to a rodeo?
Woman: No, I haven't.
Man: Well, there's one tomorrow just down there and they're great fun. You really must come.
Woman: That's a good idea. I like horses.

dialogue 1: **d)**, dialogue 2: **a)**, dialogue 3: **b)**

33 Dialogue 1:
1. He's got a new job.
2. He's got party food in his trolley.

Dialogue 2:
1. She stood on his toe.
2. England.
3. In the States.
4. It's a beautiful place and the people are so friendly. And the skiing is good.

Dialogue 3:
1. New York.
2. She's on holiday.
3. Yesterday.
4. Going to a rodeo.

34 Nice day today, isn't it? → dialogue 1
Wow. What a great view! → dialogue 3
Have a nice day. → dialogue 1
It was really nice to have met you. → dialogue 2
I just love an English accent. → dialogue 2
May I ask you where you're from? → dialogue 3
Excuse me for asking, but are you from England? → dialogue 2

35 *Man:* Well, I was driving along the Highway and looking for a gas station when suddenly this cab zoomed past me. He must have being doing a hundred. Then these police cars went past, too. It was just like in the movies.

Woman: Well, I was walking around the city centre. I was looking for some Christmas presents really when my mobile started ringing. It was Tom and he wanted to invite me to a party. So, of course, I really wanted to go but I didn't have anything to wear, so I went into a great clothes shop I know and found this great pair of trousers …

Man: USA; **words:** highway, gas station, cab, movies
Woman: Britain; **words:** city centre, mobile phone, trousers

Revision B (Unit 2–3)

1 1. B; 2. C; 3. E; 4. A; 5. F; 6. D

2 1. Quentin; 2. Mick; 3. Henry; 4. Luke; 5. Sophie; 6. Lisa; 7. Henry; 8. Sally

3 1. true; 2. true, 3. false; 4. false; 5. false; 6. true; 7. true
Korrektur:
3. Sally's dad had to move to Montana.
4. Sally and Luke didn't mind moving to Montana.
5. Sally didn't tell her mum that she had split up from her boyfriend.

4 *Henry:* I love it here. You don't know how lucky you are, Frank, to live out here.
Frank: Actually we do know. We moved out here from New York six years ago.
Henry: Did you? So why did you move out here?
Frank: Well, we came out here on holiday one winter and we loved it here so much that we decided to move.
Henry: And was it easy?
Frank: Yes, we were lucky. We found this lodge and bought it. Houses and land are a lot cheaper out here than in New York so we could sell our flat and buy all this. And it's easy to live here. We earn money from our cows and chickens and horses. And visitors come to stay out here.
Henry: And don't you miss living in New York at all?
Frank: No, we don't. Do we, Love?
Jenny: No, I can't imagine living there any more. There are just too many people and too little space in New York.
Henry: Yes, I agree with you there. But I worry about missing the theatre and the cinema out here. I mean there's not so much to do out here, is there?
Frank: Yes, you're right about the theatre and cinema but in my opinion there are enough things to do out here. I enjoy things more here because I've got more time to enjoy them. Out here you notice nature more. You notice the seasons, plants and animals and you've got time to enjoy them. In New York you don't even notice whether it's winter or summer.

Henry: Well, I'm afraid I don't agree with that. We had a lot of snow last winter.
Frank: Yes, but I mean life doesn't change because of the snow, does it? Not much, I mean. You still go to work in the subway which almost always runs and sit in your office which is always the same temperature.
Henry: Yes, I see what you mean. I've never really thought about that.
Frank: Yes, it's funny. There are lots of things you only notice when you try living in a different place.
Henry: Well, I'll look forward to finding that out then.

1. Frank and Jenny moved to Montana from **New York.**
2. They moved **six years** ago.
3. They had come out **on holiday** one winter.
4. They have **cows** and visitors at their lodge.
5. They **don't miss** their life in New York.
6. There were **too many** people in New York.
7. Frank misses **the cinema.**
8. Henry **understands** when Frank explains why you don't notice the seasons in New York.

5 Hi Sally,
I'm slowly getting used to **living here.** Everything **seemed so slow** at first. **Getting to school** takes an hour but Quentin **drives me so that's good.** I **love swimming in the** river here. And tomorrow **we're going to a rodeo.** I'm looking **forward to going** there.
CU Sally

6 *Mann:* Hi.
Du: **Hi. It's a great view up here, isn't it?**
Frau: Yes, it is. It's wonderful. And it was a hard hike up here.
Du: **Yes, it was, but it was worth it. Could you take a picture of us, please?**
Mann: Yes, of course. How does it work? OK. There you are.
Du: **Thanks very much. Excuse me for asking, but are you from around here?**
Mann: Yes, we're from Helena. We always come out to the mountains at the weekend.
Du: **Oh, that's interesting. And would you recommend seeing anywhere around here?**
Frau: Yes, I'd visit the Big Belt Mountains if I were you. They are beautiful.
Du: **Thank you. It's very nice to have met you.**

Unit 4

1 a) mountains, b) canyon, c) trail, d) river

2 1. abseiling, climbing; 2. surfing, rowing; 3. orienteering; 4. skating; 5. backpacking; 6. jogging, hiking

3 across: 1. storyline; 4. score; 5. review; 6. actor; 8. plot; 9. rating; 10. casting
down: 1. screenplay; 2. elements; 3. director; 4. screen; 7. running

4 Vorliebe – like; Freude – joy/happiness; Gefühl – feeling; Wunsch – wish; Wert – value; Angst – fear

5 1. The road is **narrow.** 2. The mountain is **high** *(auch* tall *ist möglich, aber unüblich).* 3. The man is **tall.**

6 dead – alive; nervous – brave; nice – nasty; surprising – predictable

7 help: helpless – hilflos; helpful – hilfreich
joy: joyless – freudlos; joyful – freudig, voller Freude
fear: fearless – ohne Angst, furchtlos; fearful – ängstlich
end: endless – endlos; – *(keine Bildung mit* -ful *möglich)*

8
1. When I think about jumping out of a plane, I don't think I'll be able to do it. – **The best thing to do is not to think about it.**
2. I'm too scared to climb any higher. – We're almost there now. **Just try not to look down.**
3. I'm worried that I'll forget my words again when I go on stage. – Oh, you'll be fine. **The first time is always the most difficult.**
4. I don't want to do it now. It would be awful if the rope broke. – **Don't worry about the rope breaking.** It is too strong.

9 to **criticize** a film; to **solve** a problem; to **crash** a plane; to **dig** a hole; to **pull** a bag on wheels; to **quit** a job

10 Chris loves the outdoors so when he was offered the chance **to work** in a camp in the Rockies, it wasn't difficult **to decide**. It's hard work. He must **get**

up early every day and he works till late. But in his free time he can **do** what he likes.
He's finished work when he suddenly has the idea **to walk** to the top of the mountain so that he can **see** the sunset. He forgets that he will have to **come** down again in the dark. The sunset is amazing and Chris feels happy when it's time **to go** home but when he tries **to find** the way, he can't **do** it. He has to **stay** on the mountain top all night. He's scared but when the sun comes up the next morning, he is glad that he has been such an idiot.

11

1. She wanted **to try** a new sport. → after the verb "want"
2. She went orienteering but didn't know how **to find** her way. → after a question word
3. She wondered whether **to go** left or right. → after a question word
4. She asked a girl **to show** her. → after verb + object
5. The girl showed her how **to read** a map. → after a question word
6. It was more difficult **to do** than she had thought. → after an adjective
7. She was the last one **to finish.** → after "the last"

12

1. I want my friends to come with me.
2. I'd like my holiday to be exciting.
3. I don't know how to climb.
4. I expect the teachers to teach us well.
5. I hope I won't be the only person to be scared.

13

Ella was my first friend to go on holiday alone.
She didn't know what to take with her.
We advised her to take her mobile phone and some money.
Her parents expected her to be careful.

14

I love **going/to go** to the movies. I'd love **to be** in the movies myself but I'm not very good at **acting.** Before I decide what **to watch,** I read all the reviews. That's the best way **to find** the best films, I think.
I like **buying/to buy** my ticket very early and then I go into the cinema before everybody else starts **coming/to come** in. When I'm the first person **to go** in, I can choose the best seat. I prefer **sitting/to sit** quite near the front but not too near. I have my favourite seat so I don't have to wonder where **to sit** for too long. And do you know what I really hate? I hate people **eating** (to hate *ist nicht möglich, weil es sich hier um eine Objekt + -ing-Form-Konstruktion handelt)* crisps while I'm watching the film.

15

1. I mustn't forget **to buy** her a birthday present.
2. I'll never forget **meeting** her the very first time.
3. I was playing football and I saw her when I stopped **to have** a drink.

16 1. c); 2. e); 3. a); 4. b); 5. d)

17 1.

Man: I can't go on. I can't get up any higher. I'll have to go down again.
Woman: No. Look. There to your left. Try that.
Man: OK.

2.

Woman: I need a break.
Man: Yes, OK. I'm hungry, too. Look. We can sit and eat something over there.

3.

Man: We've done it. We've done it. We've made it to the top.
Woman: Amazing. I never thought we'd do it. And just look at that view.

4.

Woman: Come on. Let's take a photo now so we can show everybody.
Man: OK. Get the camera out then.
Woman: I don't have it. Don't you have it?
Man: No. I thought you wanted to bring it.

5.

Woman: Never mind. I don't need a photo to remember this.
Man: No, it's been a great day and I won't forget it quickly.

1. He'll try **going** to the left.
2. They're going to stop **to eat** something.
3. They went on **to get** to the top.
4. They meant **to bring** the camera.
5. They'll remember **getting** to the top for a long time.

18

1. He asked her if she liked the States.
2. She answered that she had never been there.
3. He invited her to go with him.

19

1. She asked if/whether they had seen that film the summer before.
2. He answered that that film had only come out a few days before.
3. He asked when dinner would be ready.
4. She answered that they were going to buy something from a takeaway.
5. He told her to come on then and put her shoes on.

20 *Kylie:* Mum, can I go on a climbing holiday with Alex?
Mum: I don't know. Climbing is very dangerous.
Kylie: But you went climbing last year.
Mum: Yes, and it was very dangerous. How do you want to pay for it?

Kylie: I've saved enough money.
Mum: OK, you can go but you must be very careful.

Kylie asked her mum **if** she **could** go on a climbing holiday with Alex.
Her mum answered she **didn't** know and that climbing **was** very dangerous.
Kylie said that her mum **had gone** climbing **the year before.**
Her mum had agreed but said that it **had been** very dangerous.
Her mum then asked **how** she **wanted** to pay for it.
Kylie said that she **had saved** enough money.
Her Mum said OK but that she **had to** be very careful.

21 Title: A Christmas Carol
Running time: 96 minutes; Rating: PG
Director: Robert Zemeckis
Cast: Jim Carrey, Colin Firth, Bill Murray, Gary Oldman
Who is it recommended for? People who are interested in technology

22 1. fact; 2. fact; 3. fact; 4. opinion; 5. opinion; 6. opinion; 7. fact; 8. opinion

23
1. The story takes place in the **1800s** in **London.**
2. Most of the story takes place the night **before** Christmas.
3. Charles Dickens is **a writer.**
4. The four ghosts show Scrooge he needs to become **kinder.**
5. Small children aren't allowed to watch the film **without** parents.
6. The writer of the review liked **some** of the film.

24 1. A.; 2. C.; 3. B.

25 A. newspaper report; B. movie review; C. personal profile

26
1. He is an actor.
2. Climbing.
3. Because he would have called on his cell phone if he was okay.
4. Franka Potente, Moritz Bleibtreu.
5. The acting is good. The film is exciting and funny. He recommends it.
6. Two.
7. They are teachers.
8. At school.

27 Dialogue 1:

Man: Oh, I wish I hadn't agreed to do this. I'm too scared to go on. And I can't go back. The river is too strong. Can we get out and carry the canoe?

Woman: No. Just look at those rocks. But don't worry. It'll be fine. You'll be safe. It's great fun. Really! When you've done it once, you'll want to get out and do it again. I promise you.

Man: Well, I don't have a lot of choice, do I?

Woman: No. Come on. Let's go now.

Dialogue 2:

Mum: Come on. You look great. Off you go.

Boy: Oh no. I've changed my mind. I don't want to go.

Mum: Kate will be waiting for you. You have to go. And anyway you have been looking forward to going to this party with her for ages.

Boy: I know. But now I'm worried that my friends will laugh at me. They'll be there, I'm sure. And I don't want to lose my friends and I don't want Kate to think that I'm an idiot.

Mum: Well, you know your friends are jealous that they don't have a girlfriend. So the best thing to do is just to ignore them if they laugh at you and enjoy being with Kate.

Boy: That's easy for you to say.

Dialogue 3:

Girl: Oh, this is too awful. I'm going home.

Boy: No, don't go home. Come on. You can't miss this chance.

Girl: I can. When I think about it, my knees feel weak. I can't speak well. There's no way I'll be able to act.

Boy: Look! I'm sure the first time is always the worst. You need to go in there and act your part as well as you can. Even if it goes wrong, it'll be easier the next time.

Girl: Yes, but the director is really good and I'd like her to think that I'm good, too. I don't want her to think that I'm bad – I'd prefer her not to see me at all.

Dialogue 4:

Woman: No, I can't do it. I'm too scared to go over that cliff. Just look how high it is!

Man: No, don't look how high it is. Just try not to look down. You can do it.

Woman: But I don't want to do it now. Why should anybody want to go down a cliff on a rope? That's just crazy.

Man: But you'll feel better when you have done it. You'll have a lot more confidence. Come on. I'd really like you to come down with me.

a) 4.; b) 1.; c) 3.; d) 2.

28 1. dialogue 3; 2. dialogue 1; 3. dialogue 1; 4. dialogue 4; 5. dialogue 2

29 1. But don't **worry.** It'll be **fine. You'll** be safe.
2. … the best thing **to do** is just to **ignore** them if they laugh at you
3. I'm **sure** the first **time** is always the **worst.**
4. Just **try not to** look down. You can **do** it.

30 1. a); 2. b); 3. a), c); 4. b), c); 5. a), c); 6. b); 7. c)

Revision C (Standards)

1 1. B; 2. C; 3. D; 4. A

2 1. From London to New York.
2. At 3 am.
3. Places he had seen in films, lots of people, lots of cars.
4. Hot.
5. Baseball.
6. Their accents.
7. They grew it themselves.
8. The Grand Canyon, San Francisco and Los Angeles.
9. Actress.
10. Six weeks.

3 My friend Matt ~~flew~~ → **drove** across America this year with his parents and he really ~~hated~~ → **enjoyed/loved** it. He said that it's true that New York never sleeps because there are ~~never~~ → **always** lots of people around. He said it was exciting and ~~dangerous~~ → **safe** there. After New York he visited ~~friends~~ → **cousins** in Chicago and he loved swimming in the ~~sea~~ → **lake** there. In Los Angeles he saw Cheryl Lacey in a ~~film~~ → **café**. He said that he was glad he had visited because now he knew that the USA ~~was~~ → **wasn't** full of police officers, film stars and cowboys and Indians.

4 Hi Jeanie,
I'm fine, thanks, and I had a great holiday in England. My auntie lives in Manchester and we visited Wales, too. Everywhere we visited people spoke with a different accent and I couldn't understand them. I hope I can understand you. In England we watched some cricket matches. Is that like baseball?
I'm really excited about my holiday in Chicago. My plane lands on August 10th at 17:30. Will you be able to pick us up? I eat everything and my parents are going to stay until the 14th if that is OK.
CU next week.
Mara.

5 Hi Jeanie. It's Matt here. We're in Missouri now and I can't find my mobile. Did I leave it at your house? Could you call me back, please? On my dad's mobile.

Hello. It's Mara's father here. I'm sorry but I've had a problem at work and we can't come now until August 12th. Is that OK? Please call back soon because I need to change the flight. Thanks.

Hi Jeanie. It's Sara here. I'm at the beach house. Do you want to come and stay tomorrow for two days? You can call me at the beach house. The number is 745 39812. Hope to see you then.

1. He's lost his mobile.
2. Call his dad's mobile.
3. Mara's father.
4. At work.
5. Change the flight.
6. To invite Jeanie to stay with her at the beach house for two days.
7. 745 39812.

6

1. Oh, I'm terribly sorry. I didn't see you.
2. Can I help you with your bags?
3. Excuse me. Could you help me, please? I'm looking for the information desk./Excuse me. Could you tell me where the information desk is, please?
4. Thank you very much. You have been a great help.

1.
Man: Ow. You just stood on my toe.
You: Oh. I'm terribly sorry. I didn't see you.

2.
You: Can I help you with your bags?
Woman: Oh yes, that's very kind of you. Thank you.

3.
You: Excuse me. Could you help me, please? I'm looking for the information desk./Excuse me. Could you tell me where the information desk is, please?
Man: Yes, I can show you if you like. It's just over there.
You: Thank you very much. You have been a great help.
Man: You're welcome.

7 B.

8 1. not in text (she moved from New York but it didn't say if she had always lived there); 2. true; 3. true. 4. true; 5. false; 6. true; 7. false; 8. false; 9. true; 10. true

Korrektur:
5. She had breaks more often because she was worse at skiing.
7. Alice didn't know which way to go because she couldn't see the way.
8. She skied off the slope because she couldn't see the slope.

9 **Mountain Rescue**
Last night just after 1 o'clock Alice Baker was rescued from Erik's Mountain after a skiing accident in which she broke her leg and lost her way. She is now recovering in hospital but is expected to be allowed home later today. The accident happened just after 4 pm yesterday afternoon when she was skiing down ski slopes with four friends. They skied into a cloud and Alice fell. Her friends noticed that she was missing and went back to look for her but couldn't find her anywhere. They skied to the bottom of the mountain and waited for her there and when she did not arrive, they called the rescue number. Alice had carried on skiing but had turned the wrong way, fallen down a small cliff and hit her leg on a tree. Alice tied her leg up like she had seen in films and then skied down the mountain on one ski. A rescue helicopter found her about 1 am when she used her camera to flash into the sky.

10
Vater: Frag sie bitte, ob wir uns dazusetzen können.
Du: **Excuse me. Could we sit here, please?**
Frau: Yes, of course. May I ask you where you are from?
Du: **We're from South Germany.**
Frau: Oh, that's interesting. You're a long way from home.
Du: **Yes, but we heard that the Rockies are good for skiing.**
Frau: Yes, that's right. And do you like it here?
Mutter: Ja. Und die Pisten sind fantastisch und die Leute freundlich.
Du: **Yes, we do. The slopes are fantastic and the people are really friendly.**

11
Jody: Hello. Do you mind if I sit here?
Alice: No, not at all. I'll just move my bag. There's a fantastic view up here, isn't there?
Jody: Yes, I always feel happiest when I'm up here. Excuse me for asking but where are you from?
Alice: I'm from New York. And you? Are you from here?
Jody: Yes, I am. I've always lived around here.
Alice: And do you often go skiing?
Jody: Yes, I do. I've been skiing here since I was a little child.
Alice: So you must be good then?
Jody: Yes, I am. Or I was. I once trained in the Olympics team.
Alice: Did you? Wow, that's exciting. What was that like?

Jody: Well, I didn't actually ski in the Olympics because I had an accident before they started and broke my leg.
Alice: Oh no. That's terrible. That must have been very disappointing.
Jody: It was at the time. But you know some things seem to happen for the best. And I met the man who I later married in hospital so I soon felt happier.
Alice: And how did you have the accident?
Jody: Well, there are lots of reasons but mainly I think, I was just too tired. It was the last run of the day and I should have finished before. Yes, you must remember: the last run is always the most dangerous.
Alice: Thanks. I'll remember that.

1. Since she was a child.
2. The Olympics.
3. She broke her leg.
4. The man who she later married.

Unit 5

1 California is in the southwest of the USA and has a **border** with Mexico to the south. It has the highest **population** of all the American states because it has some very big cities and it is the third largest state. Its **climate** is very mixed with the areas near the coast wetter and cooler than those to the east. California is a very beautiful state with a fantastic **stretch** of coast in the west, mountains in the middle and a **desert** in the east. The many national parks in California have kept much of the land in its natural **state.** California's **economy** is usually one of the strongest in the world but the **standard** of living in California is also very mixed. Many people have become very rich from the **electronics** business or from their **fame** in the world of films and they live in **luxury** but many others, especially illegal immigrants, don't have enough to eat.

2 ugly: attractive, pretty, beautiful
well: poorly, badly
clever: stupid, silly
strange: familiar, normal

3

E	**X**	**C**	**L**	**U**	**S**	**I**	**V**	**E**	Z	**P**
P	A	**R**	Z	R	K	**L**	P	J	H	**R**
A	U	**I**	C	**G**	**O**	**L**	**D**	**E**	**N**	**I**
I	V	**M**	H	I	A	**E**	H	D	F	**V**
N	K	**I**	P	Z	R	**G**	E	F	C	**A**
F	O	**N**	A	D	D	**A**	**D**	**U**	**L**	**T**
U	**C**	**A**	**S**	**U**	**A**	**L**	D	R	I	**E**
L	M	**L**	N	X	S	L	Z	C	R	K

It's **illegal** to steal.
It's **criminal** to waste water in California but not always illegal.

Are you going to wear **casual** clothes to the party?
I don't think it's fair to have **private** beaches – they should be for everybody.
I love **golden** sandy beaches.
When sand is very hot, it is **painful** to walk on it.
People don't always become more **adult** when they get older.
That's a very **exclusive** restaurant – we can't eat there.

4 belassen – to keep; unterstützen –to support; anziehen – to attract; bewachen – to guard; genehmigen – to authorize; anstarren – to stare at; gießen – to water; fallen lassen – to drop; verschwenden – to waste; sausen – to speed; annehmen – to accept; fluchen – to swear; danken – to thank

5 I have never been involved **in** politics at all but I do love surfing so when a friend called **about** a meeting on a beach, I was the first to show **up.** The beach was public until a rich film star bought the land. The first we knew was when they closed **off** the beach last week. Somebody had already built a fence and put **up** a sign which said it was illegal to step **on** the beach. We had a party on the beach that night and we stayed **out/up** until the morning. It turned **out** to be the best party I've ever been to. We're going to work now until the beach is made public again. I never knew that politics was such fun.

6

1. I **got up** yesterday – late –, ran to the bus stop, **got on** the bus. I only realized it was Saturday when I **got to** school.
   get up – aufstehen; get on – einsteigen; get to – ankommen
2. I went home, **took off** my school clothes and **took out** the dog for a walk.
   take off – ausziehen; take out – ausführen
3. That evening I watched a film I hoped was a comedy but it **turned out** to be a thriller and very scary. When the hero **turned into** a monster, I **turned off** the TV and called a friend.
   to turn out (to be) – sich herausstellen (als); to turn into – sich verwandeln in; to turn off – ausschalten
4. I called Ann and asked her to **come over.** She answered that she'd like to but her cousin was staying with her. I said that the cousin should **come along,** too. Five minutes later the door bell rang and I told them to **come in.**
   to come over – herüberkommen, vorbeischauen; to come along – mitkommen; to come in – hereinkommen

7

1. Nice to meet you.
2. I'm sorry, could you repeat that, please?
3. Hello, could I speak to Ella, please?
4. Excuse me, could you help me, please?

8
1. Hey, the line starts back there.
2. Don't you know it's rude to stare?
3. What are you doing there?

9
Orlando: Hey, is that the actress **who** was in "Titanic"?
Cherry: You're right. Was "Titanic" that film **which** won lots of Oscars?
Orlando: Yes, and it was one of the first films **which/–** I saw at the movies.
Cherry: It was a true story about a ship **which** sank, wasn't it?
Orlando: Yes, and there was a captain **who** went down with his ship.
Cherry: And wasn't there a band **which** played while the ship went down?
Orlando: That's something **which/–** I couldn't do.
Cherry: But I wouldn't like to be a person **who** dies a hero.
Orlando: No. I just want to be the person **who** is the hero in the film.

10
1. Jorge, who is from Mexico, is an immigrant.
2. He lives in San Diego, which is near the Mexican border.
3. He first got a job, which was poorly paid, as a fruit picker./He first got a job as a fruit picker, which was poorly paid.
4. Jorge learnt English from a friend, whose mother was American.
5. Jorge and Ramon, who is from Chile, now have their own language school.

11
1. Many people who live in California speak Spanish and English. → *defining relative clause*
2. The Spanish which people speak in Mexico is different to the Spanish which people speak in Spain. → *defining relative clause*
3. My friends**,** who are bilingual**,** say Spanish grammar is a little like English grammar. → *non-defining relative clause*
4. English**,** which was a German language**,** has many words which are like Spanish words because they both come from Latin. → *non-defining relative clause* und *defining relative clause*

12
Hollywood**, which** is a part of Los Angeles**,** is known as the centre of the American movie industry. A lot of the industry**, which** has grown a lot since it started**,** has moved to neighbouring areas but there are still many old theatres there**(,) which** *(kann* defining *und* non-defining *sein)* are used for premiers of shows, for example. Hollywood**, which** was then a little village**,** was first used as an area to make films in 1910 by the director D. W. Griffith**, who** was actually from New York. The people **who** lived in Hollywood were so friendly that Griffith decided to make lots of other films there. The first movie studio**, which** was called Nester Studio**,** was built in Hollywood in 1911 by a company **whose** parent company also came from the east of the USA. Since that time many actors and actresses **who** want to become famous have moved to Hollywood.

13 1. People often see **surprising** things in Malibu. The people are **surprised.**
2. There are many **thrilled** visitors in Malibu. Malibu is **thrilling.**
3. People watch **exciting** surfing competitions. The people are **excited.**
4. But sometimes there are **shocking** accidents. The visitors are **shocked.**

14 My friend was never the most **exciting** person around. He was a **thinking** person and so you never found him with the **surfing** crowd. He was a much **loved** person because he was very **caring.** He was also a **reading** person who read any kind of book he found but he wasn't very **interested** in the movies. So you can imagine how **surprised** I was when he told me that he had got a part in a film. He's a **well-known** actor now but he hasn't changed at all. He's still quiet.

15 1. What a boring day!
2. I'm bored.
3. Nothing exciting will happen today.
4. There are no interesting people here.
5. I'm well-known and I'm only interested in other exciting people like me.

16 1. Arnold Schwarzenegger; 2. an Austrian village; 3. his films; 4. when he was a teenager

17 *Reihenfolge:* 3 – 1 – 4 – 2 – 9 – 5 – 8 – 7 – 6

18 1. a), c); 2. a); 3. a), b); 4. a), b); 5. a), c); 6. a), c); 7. b), c); 8. a), b), c); 9. a), b); 10. c)

19 Setting: beach in California
Characters: Daniel (beginner surfer), Janice (girlfriend), lifeguards
Plot: Daniel goes surfing. Janice watches from beach. Janice sees shark, Daniel doesn't. Daniel disappears. Janice sees Daniel on beach.
Atmosphere: first: fun, later: exciting, scary

20 "Can I take you anywhere?" called José out of his window. Carla looked at him and wasn't sure. She had just had big problems with men who had wanted to help her. But she couldn't walk forever along this hot, dry road. She went to the car and got in.
Carla's English wasn't very good but they managed to talk. They talked, but didn't tell the truth. Carla didn't tell José that she was an illegal immigrant, who had just crossed the border, and José didn't tell her that he was a well-known actor. Carla liked José and was just beginning to relax when she saw a police car in front of them. She was scared. They would want to see her papers and they would send her back.

Jose looked at her and realized the truth. When the police stopped them, Carla got a surprise. “Hello, José Garcia. Wow. Nice to meet you! Can you please sign an autograph for my wife? She won’t believe me when I tell her I met you.”
José smiled, signed an autograph and introduced his new girlfriend, Carla. Then they drove on. “Thank you,” said Carla, and then it was time for the truth.

21 Dialogue 1:

Mr Jenkins:	Hello?
John:	Hello. Er. Could I speak to Lewis, please?
Mr Jenkins:	No, I’m sorry. Lewis isn’t here at the moment. He’s at baseball training, I think. He should be back in an hour or so.
John:	Oh, I’ll be out then. Could you give him a message for me, please?
Mr Jenkins:	Yes, of course. What should I tell him? Is that John?
John:	Yes. It’s me. Er. Could you tell him that I won’t be able to come round tonight? I’ve got to finish an article for the school newspaper.
Mr Jenkins:	Yes, OK. And do you want him to call you back?
John:	Er. Yes, if he’s got time to help me, then that would be great.
Mr Jenkins:	OK then, John. Good luck with your article.
John:	Thank you, Mr Jenkins. Goodbye.

Dialogue 2:

Liz:	Hello.
Paul:	Hi, Liz. It’s Paul. Have you been watching the news?
Liz:	No, I’m at the pool. Why? What’s happened?
Paul:	There’s been a small earthquake in San Francisco and I …
Liz:	Oh my God. Louise and Jane are there. What are we going to do? We’ve got to drive over there now. We’ve got to go and rescue them. They’ll be …
Paul:	Liz, would you shut up for two seconds. Just calm down. I’ve already spoken to them and they’re fine.
Liz:	Oh. Why didn’t you tell me that right away? Why did you scare me like that? My heart almost stopped. You almost …
Paul:	Liz. Liz you didn’t let me finish. Just listen for a little while.. They want to come home early because their hostel has been damaged and they haven’t got anywhere to stay, so they’ll be arriving home tomorrow evening.
Liz:	Oh, oh great. Thanks for phoning, Paul.

Dialogue 3:

Woman:	Hello. Can I help you, please?
Girl:	Hello. Yes, we’re visiting San Francisco for five days and we want to know what there is to do around here.

Woman: Well, you can do almost anything in San Francisco and you could stay here for a year and not see everything so first of all tell me what you're interested in. Are you interested in museums, for example?
Girl: Yes, we are. We're interested in art.
Woman: Then you must visit the Museum of Modern Art.
Girl: Is it easy to find?
Woman: Yes. Look! I'll give you a map. There it is and here we are.
Girl: Great. Thank you. And we'd like to go to the beach. Which beaches would you recommend?
Woman: Er, do you want to go surfing?
Girl: No, we just want to relax and go swimming.
Woman: Well, the Pacific is really quite cold here at this time of year. Are you planning to go south at all?
Girl: Yes, we're going to travel to Los Angeles next.
Woman: Well, if I were you, I'd wait until you got there before you hit the beach. There are lots of other things to do in San Francisco and some wonderful parks to relax in.
Girl: Thanks very much.

Dialogue 4:
Tricia: Hi, Kevin. Come in. You're early.
Kevin: Hi Tricia. I thought we might have a chance to chat before the others get here.
Tricia: Do you want to put your bag in there? And get yourself a drink if you want one. You know where they are.
Kevin: Thanks. Tricia. Can I get you something?
Tricia: No, but can you give me a hand with this table? I want to put it outside and then I can put some food and drink out there. It's such a beautiful day, we can go in the garden.
Kevin: Yeah, good idea. Where are your parents? Have they gone out for the evening?
Tricia: Yes, they're visiting my grandparents.
Kevin: And do they know you're having a party?
Tricia: Well, they know I've invited a few friends around.
Kevin: A few? You're invited all our class, haven't you?
Tricia: Yes, well. Forty or a few? What's the difference?

1. polite; 2. casual; 3. polite; 4. casual

22 A. 4; B. 2; C. 1; D. 3

23 Can I get you something? → dialogue 4
Oh my God. → dialogue 2
Can I help you, please? → dialogue 3

Could I speak to Lewis, please? → dialogue 1
No, but can you give me a hand with this table? → dialogue 4
And do you want him to call you back? → dialogue 1
Which beaches would you recommend? → dialogue 3
Liz, would you shut up for two seconds. → dialogue 2
Could you give him a message for me, please? → dialogue 1
And get yourself a drink if you want one. → dialogue 4

24 Dialogue 1: 1. At baseball training. 2. In an hour or so. 3. He's got to finish an article for the school newspaper. 4. Yes, if he has time to help.
Dialogue 2: 1. There's been an earthquake. 2. In San Francisco. 3. Their hostel has been damaged. 4. Tomorrow evening.
Dialogue 3: 1. Five days. 2. Museums and beaches. 3. The water's too cold. 4. Los Angeles.
Dialogue 4: 1. He wanted to chat. 2. A table. 3. Visiting her grandparents. 4. No, they don't.